RELATIONSHIP REPAIR

Quizzes, Exercises, Advice & Affirmations
to Mend Any Matter of the Heart

by Robin Westen

STERLING INNOVATION
An imprint of Sterling Publishing Co., Inc.

New York / London
www.sterlingpublishing.com

STERLING, the Sterling logo, STERLING INNOVATION, and the Sterling Innovation
logo are registered trademarks of Sterling Publishing Co., Inc.

10 9 8 7 6 5 4 3 2 1

Published by Sterling Publishing Co., Inc.
387 Park Avenue South, New York, NY 10016
© 2010 by Sterling Publishing Co., Inc.

Distributed in Canada by Sterling Publishing   —
c/o Canadian Manda Group, 165 Dufferin Street
Toronto, Ontario, Canada M6K 3H6
Distributed in the United Kingdom by GMC Distribution Services
Castle Place, 166 High Street, Lewes, East Sussex, England BN7 1XU
Distributed in Australia by Capricorn Link (Australia) Pty. Ltd.
P.O. Box 704, Windsor, NSW 2756, Australia

Sterling ISBN 978-1-4027-7035-7

Design by Alicia Freile, Tango Media

For information about custom editions, special sales, premium and
corporate purchases, please contact Sterling Special Sales
Department at 800-805-5489 or specialsales@sterlingpublishing.com.

To the incomparable Heart Sutra

Contents

Introduction 6

Section One: Quizzes

Section Two: Healing

Section Three: Journal

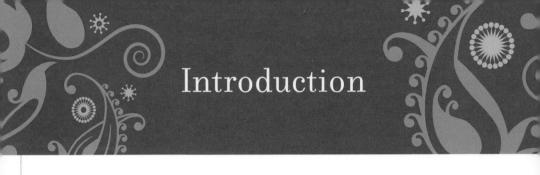

Introduction

My friend Clarice is vice president of a leading media corporation and as anyone would guess, a charming, self-sufficient, resourceful, and decisive woman. But when it comes to a three-year relationship with her partner, Stuart, she sways like a willow in the Caribbean breeze. "I don't know if it's worth keeping him around," she laments one day. The next? "I can't live without the guy." Two days later, it's, "We're fighting all the time . . . What's the point?"

Well, one thing is for sure: Clarice isn't alone. Lots of us are angsting over our relationships. According to a study at the University of Utah, of 276 couples interviewed, almost one-third reported being unhappy with their relationship. And in another survey, four in ten American women admitted if they had to do it over again—they *wouldn't*. Yet, you're still hanging in there. What gives?

Just like most things in life, relationships are complicated. Biologically speaking, at the start, there's the unmistakable and unshakable endorphin rush—the release of a feel-good brain chemical—that makes us literally blinded by love. Interestingly, when it comes to love at first sight, men are the most susceptible and spontaneous. Researchers found guys can fall in love after only 8.2 seconds; it takes women on average, five times longer. Still, regardless of sex, there's not much chance to reflect on what's turning us on. No matter how momentary a reaction, once we're head over heels in love, we see nothing in front of us but a lifetime of hot sex, eye-to-eye contact, comforting support, and deep, endearing communication.

According to scientists, this romantic rush lasts approximately three months. Then there's the honeymoon period. Even if the initial jolt of endorphins has eased, we're still entranced, or at least willing to suspend doubts. But between six months and a year later, most of us are haunted by these doubts. In fact, *filled* with them. Suddenly, Mr. Wonderful isn't such a good listener, takes us for granted, is too touchy or an insensitive lug, spends all his free time with friends or hangs around moping, is a know-it-all or too indecisive, can't get along with our family members, or panders, bullies, or quakes, forgets to put his socks away, leaves the bathroom mirror streaked, ignores our G-spot, overlooks Valentine's Day . . . Well, the list of complaints goes on. We wonder whether it's worth it. Should we stay together, or are the problems too damaging? Is it better to cut our losses now and split? Or can we salvage all the good stuff and work on what's souring the partnership?

That's where *Relationship Repair* comes to the rescue.

Relationship Repair is a workbook, venting diary, healing guide, diagnostic tool, and inspirational manual. It takes participants through the different dynamics of their relationship, covering areas such as:

- How much a couple knows about each other
- Their compatibility as a couple
- Their level of commitment
- Their argument styles
- Whether they can forgive past hurts

It also mines a duo's weaknesses as well as enduring strengths, and it measures overall happiness. Through the use of quizzes, questionnaires, affirmations, and exercises, couples can discover where they come together and where they fall apart. It gives partners guidance on how to heal and keep their relationship healthy.

After each quiz is taken and scored, there is a pointed analysis, followed by advice on how to repair problems. Although the exercises are practical, there are no quick fixes; they require time and commitment. But here's the good news: Many relationships are worth saving. After all, how often do we *really* fall in love or think we do?

Relationship Repair is also packed with the latest research to support its program. It covers subjects like love at first sight, whether opposites really attract, why we fall in love with people who are unavailable, the most effective way to argue, as well as other research-based reports. Throughout the book, expert advice from leading authorities in the field of relationships is offered, and there's room at the end to write down your thoughts, ponder progress, and note areas that still need improvement. In addition, there are helpful affirmations to nurture the healing work and a checklist of key components *all* healthy relationships possess. Readers can use the checklist to acknowledge progress as their relationship evolves and improves. Included are quotes from wise minds to help inspire and lead couples in a new and more loving direction. The final section is a journal where you can write down your thoughts as your relationship grows and changes.

We *can* heal our relationships, but it's important to use both our hearts and our minds in the process. That's how *Relationship Repair* helps readers to become reasoned and rational as well as to exercise their heart muscles. For example, when your mind tells you to remember past hurts, listen to your heart and work on letting them go. When your mind tells you to hang on to the past, listen to your heart and work on forgiveness. Since carrying around old pain and anger only leads to anxiety and depression, readers receive tools on how to forgive and move on. The exercises throughout this book help release what is toxic and no longer needed. Ultimately, *Relationship Repair* brings participants to a stronger connection; renewed romance; and solid, sustainable love.

Whole and thriving relationships bring endless happiness and health to our lives. Countless studies show that people with healthy relationships possess a higher level of optimism and quantitatively less stress. There *are* proven ways to make relationships work. When readers follow the course in *Relationship Repair*, they will find themselves inhabiting a new romantic landscape with an open and energized outlook.

Good luck and good love.

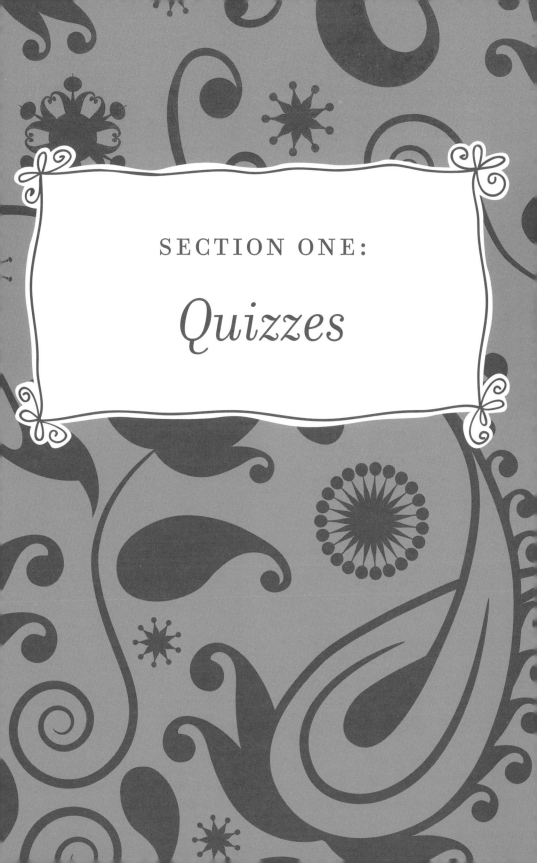

SECTION ONE:

Quizzes

Chapter One:
Know Thyself

Which Personality Type Is Your Perfect Match?

Sure, he makes your knees weak and your heart pound, but that doesn't mean he's a keeper. We're often attracted to certain men because they trigger unresolved issues, which can make the relationship seem nonstop exciting or cozily familiar. Either way, think about how it feels when you scratch poison ivy: short-term pleasure—long-term aggravation. To reach a healthy place in a relationship, you need to recognize the personality type that enhances the *best* parts of you, plays down your weaknesses, and ultimately makes you feel good about yourself. Take this test and identify the kind of man who not only rocks your world, but who also offers the kind of support it takes to build a lasting foundation.

PART ONE Mark the statement that you most agree with:

1

a. I believe in fate.

b. I believe we control our own destinies.

c. I believe it's all a lot of hooey.

2

a. You can change someone through the power of love.

b. We're the only ones who can make changes in ourselves.

c. Change is an illusion.

3

a. Love makes the world go 'round.

b. Money makes the world go 'round.

c. Action makes the world go 'round.

4

a. We're attracted to our soul mates.

b. Opposites attract.

c. Attraction is bio-chemical.

5

a. I can read someone's true nature in an instant.

b. It takes time to get to know someone.

c. We never really know anybody.

PART TWO Complete the following:

6 **To win the support for a project that's close to your heart, would you:**

a. Appeal to an audience's humanitarian impulses with an impassioned speech.

b. Organize and circulate a petition to support your cause.

c. Prove it can work with facts and figures.

7 The supermarket's gourmet section is promoting some mouth-watering (but rather expensive) goodies. You're more likely to:

a. Treat yourself to the tastiest item.

b. Make do with a few samples.

c. Pass it up—you don't want to be tempted.

8 In your dream biopic, which of these hunks would you never cast as your leading man?

a. George Clooney

b. Hugh Jackman

c. Brad Pitt

9 Your man could make your heart sing the loudest by:

a. Offering you a perfect red rose with a graceful flourish.

b. Fixing all the leaky faucets in the house—without making you ask even once.

c. Balancing a budget.

10 You prefer your days to be:

a. Open—so you can meet situations spontaneously as they arise.

b. Busy—but with free time for friends and family.

c. Totally booked—you like to carefully plan your time well in advance.

11 What guides you most when it comes to making important decisions?

a. Following your own beliefs

b. Being as fair as possible to others

c. Proven facts

Analysis

Note: If your score falls equally between two categories, read both descriptions since you may share characteristics of each type.

MOSTLY A'S
YOUR HEART RULES.

A real romantic, you're in love with love, and because you're ultra-sensitive you laugh and cry at the slightest provocation. Even though to the outside world you may sometimes appear to be a bit over-the-top, your reactions are 100 percent genuine. Your charm lies in the fact that your heart is an open book—but the downside is that it leaves you susceptible to all kinds of drama in your relationships.

ADVICE

Look for a guy with two feet firmly planted on the ground to counteract your tendency to fall prey to emotional highs and lows. A rooted guy will help you stay balanced—but don't go for a hard heart. You'll want someone who appreciates your sensitivity but knows how to remain calm in a storm.

MOSTLY B'S
YOU'RE BALANCED.

We're not talking about Evel Knievel, but your perfect match is a man willing to go out on a limb for you—and let you know that some risks are worth taking. Why? A bit of a wimp, you're most passionate about being sensible. Of course it's a good idea to be cautious, but too much caution can close you down to some of life's real pleasures.

ADVICE

A man who is spontaneous, effusive, full of energy, and knows how to have a good time is the guy for you. Don't be afraid to let yourself be swept off your feet. Your ultimate romantic happiness requires that you take a chance on love.

MOSTLY C'S
YOUR INTELLECT TAKES THE LEAD.

Ms. *Brainiac*, most of the decisions you make are based on facts and there's no arguing this kind of thinking has done you well. Friends and colleagues come to you for advice and you give them the lowdown based on solid research and sure-footed statistics. It's natural with this kind of solid mind-set to look for a match who sees the world the same way you do. But when it comes to love, that's not always the right answer.

ADVICE

You'll do well with a man who looks to the heavens and has some faith in what can't be proven. Your perfect match may be a philosopher, a poet, or a plumber who ponders the universe—anyone who reaches your depths and expands your horizons.

Exercise

Ask these crucial questions:

- Is he honest? You need someone who doesn't lie, weasel, or fudge issues.
- Is he reliable? You want someone doing what he says he would do when he said he would do it.
- Is he emotionally open? Or does he need a sledgehammer to get him to admit his feelings?
- Is he kind and considerate to you, his friends, and his family?
- Does he need alcohol, drugs, or constant approval to bolster his confidence?

"Sometimes if you're lucky, someone comes into your life who'll take up a place in your heart that no one else can fill; someone who's tighter than a twin, more with you than your own shadow, who gets deeper under your skin than your own blood and bones."

—SNOOP DOGG

What's Your Relationship Style?

"When it comes to relationships, most of us fall into one of four categories," says Greg Godek, author of the best-selling *1001 Ways to Be Romantic*. This quiz will identify *your* relationship style and tell you how to make the most of what works for you.

1 Of these, the gift you would most like to get from your honey is a:
a. Big box of assorted chocolates.
b. Night out on the town.
c. Spa vacation.
d. Dozen long-stem roses.

2 Your favorite shade of blue is:
a. Baby blue.
b. Electric blue.
c. Powder blue.
d. Turquoise.

3 What do you usually wear when you're just hanging around the house?
a. Silky lingerie
b. Sweatpants
c. Bathrobe
d. Jeans and a T-shirt

4 Which of these style homes can you see yourself in?
a. Victorian
b. Ranch
c. Colonial
d. Modern

5 Pick the bouquet you would like by your bedside.

a. Birds-of-paradise

b. Wildflowers

c. Roses

d. Orchids

6 How would you show your man you care?

a. I'd send him an erotic text.

b. I'd write "I love you" on the bathroom mirror.

c. I'd cook his favorite dinner.

d. I'd give him a night of lovemaking he'd never forget.

7 Imagine the most comfy date you could share with your guy. It would be:

a. A candlelit dinner.

b. Watching a scary movie together.

c. Curled up by the fire sharing a bottle of wine.

d. Lying in your bathing suits under a sizzling sun.

8 Which of these golden oldie songs most closely describes your sentiments?

a. "At Last" by Etta James

b. "Till There Was You" by The Beatles

c. "Ain't No Mountain High Enough" by Diana Ross

d. "In Your Eyes" by Peter Gabriel

Analysis

MOSTLY A'S
YOUR RELATIONSHIP STYLE IS BOLD AND FIERY.

Strong, flirtatious, and ultra-feminine, when it comes to relationships, you know what you want and never settle for anything less. "You know how to turn on the charm—and love to keep your man guessing," says Godek.

ADVICE

Encourage your partner to participate in making decisions—big and small. That way, he'll not only feel valued, but he'll take on more responsibility, too.

Begin sentences by saying "I feel . . ." instead of "You don't . . ." This approach guarantees conversations that are give-and-take, so you both get to weigh in.

MOSTLY B'S
YOUR RELATIONSHIP STYLE IS PLAYFUL AND ENERGETIC.

Outgoing, free-spirited, and spontaneous, you follow wherever your romantic impulses lead. That includes shouting "I love you!" from the rooftop—even if your guy is a little less public about his feelings. "Your free spirit also means you accept your partner as is—and insist on the same," says Godek.

ADVICE

Tune in to your partner's moods—even if that means opting for a quiet evening at home rather than a night on the town.

Try planning ahead sometimes. It ensures you'll find time to connect—and lets you zero in on things you *both* enjoy!

MOSTLY C'S
YOUR RELATIONSHIP STYLE IS STRAIGHTFORWARD AND SIMPLE.

Matter-of-fact and easy to get along with, you let the little disputes roll off your back because you want life to be uncomplicated. "This approach can keep stress at bay—as long as you're not stifling your true feelings just to keep the peace," says Godek.

ADVICE

Learn to speak your mind. Psychologists say this takes practice, so begin with small issues and build confidence.

Treat yourself! Nothing extravagant—maybe a bubble bath—just a reminder that your needs and wants also deserve attention!

MOSTLY D'S
YOUR RELATIONSHIP IS WILD AND PASSIONATE.

A die-hard romantic, your undying faith in the power of love and relationship means you'll risk it *all* for matters of the heart. "Leading such an emotional-centered life makes you sensitive," says Godek. The result: You may perceive a slight where none was intended and react in a flash and way too harshly.

ADVICE

Name your feelings. This helps work through complicated emotions.

Spend fifteen minutes moving. Just that much exercise or alone time can keep your emotions steady.

Piglet sidled up to Pooh from behind.
"Pooh!" he whispered. "Yes, Piglet?"
"Nothing," said Piglet, taking Pooh's paw.
"I just wanted to be sure of you."

—A.A. MILNE

Are You Happy with Yourself?

These inkblots reveal the writing on the wall!

For decades, psychologists have used the inkblot test to analyze personalities. Now you can take this simple test to discover just how happy you are with yourself—and learn easy ways to boost your self-esteem.

INSTRUCTIONS:

Take a minute to look at the inkblot and get a clear impression before moving on to each question.

IMAGE A

1 **How does this image make you feel?**

a. Calm and rested

b. Happy or exuberant

c. Curious or restless

2 **What is the strongest image you see in the inkblot?**

a. Diamond, jewel, or flower

b. Insect or bird

c. Airplane or spaceship

3 **This inkblot seems like it could be:**

a. Ancient or from the past.

b. Current.

c. Futuristic.

IMAGE B

4 What's the *first* thing you see?

a. Eyes

b. A cape, robe, or coat

c. Wings

5 This image seems:

a. Feminine.

b. Masculine.

c. Neither feminine nor masculine.

6 Of these emotions, what does the inkblot most strongly convey?

a. Happiness

b. Pride

c. Readiness for action

IMAGE C

7 Try to find two insects in this inkblot. What are they doing?

a. Kissing

b. Dancing

c. Flying

8 Imagine the insects are speaking. They are talking about their:

a. Romantic feelings for each other.

b. Hopes and dreams.

c. Plans or directions for a big trip.

9 What bothers you about this picture?

a. Nothing

b. It's not exactly the same on both sides.

c. The insects look too flat.

Analysis

MOSTLY A'S
YOU'RE COMFORTABLE IN YOUR OWN SKIN.

Your interpretation of these inkblots shows that your inner world is just fine the way it is. This is great news because it means you rate high in optimism and overall life satisfaction—which naturally keeps stress at bay. What's your secret? You accept life as it comes, roll with the punches, and appreciate simple pleasures like time with family and friends. It doesn't mean you don't strive for self-improvement. Of course you do! But every step of the way you stay patient—and know how to reward yourself for every job well done!

MOSTLY B'S
YOU'D LIKE TO SHAKE THINGS UP—BUT JUST A LITTLE.

Even though you love your life, the way you see the images reveals that every now and then you want to tweak it. Go ahead! You deserve a break, whether that means making time for a relaxing bath, walking with friends, taking a stroll through the mall, or having a night out dancing. To rattle your *cage* a bit, consider changing your haircut or color, moving the furniture around at home, or simply wearing a different lipstick shade. Studies show even little changes like these will put a new bounce in your step!

MOSTLY C'S
YOU CRAVE A BIG ADVENTURE!

Your inkblot answers reveal your innate zest for life, natural curiosity, and openness to possibilities. You want to explore the unknown, embrace challenges, and set the bar higher. The truth is, there's nothing holding you back! Your great adventure can take place right here and now even with family and responsibilities. Take a risk by plunging into a creative activity like writing a book or painting, meeting new friends, or exploring unknown neighborhoods. Sometimes the greatest adventure takes place in your own mind—so let your daydreams soar!

Advice

It's natural to believe all we need to be happy is to find someone with whom to share our life. If only relationships were that simple. Countless studies have shown that the happiest and most enduring couples are those who feel confident and fulfilled all by themselves. That's why, before you set your sights on romance, it's important to get in touch with what *you* desire from life—and then create the attitude to make it happen. The truth is, you want someone who feels happy and secure within themselves. *Right?* Well, your perfect partner will look for the same. In other words, don't search for the missing piece. Before committing to a relationship, find out what brings you joy, go for it, and be whole and happy on your own.

Exercises

BOOST YOUR SELF-ESTEEM: MAKE SOME LISTS

- Five of your strengths—for example, persistence, courage, friendliness, creativity
- Five things you admire about yourself—for example, the way you have good relationships with friends
- Five of the greatest achievements in your life
- At least twenty accomplishments (they can be as simple as learning to knit or as admirable as reading the complete works of Proust)
- Ten things you could do to help someone else

MORNING AFFIRMATIONS

- I deserve to be happy and successful.
- I can make my own decisions.
- I can choose happiness over misery.
- I can be confident.
- I deserve to be truly loved.

"Once we believe in ourselves, we can risk curiosity, wonder, spontaneous delight, or any experience that reveals the human spirit."

—E.E. CUMMINGS

Find Out How Well Your Partner Really Knows You!

Few of us believe our partners know *everything* about us—and that's a good thing. A certain air of mystery is essential for keeping interest and sexual tension alive. He doesn't need to know, for example, every page in *every* chapter in your sexual history book. But it's important that your partner truly *gets* the essential core of your being. It's the way, experts say, we develop real intimacy and relationship resilience. What's *most* crucial to know? Your values, priorities, and basic views on life are essential. This quiz will reveal just how much your partner knows about you and vice versa.

Caveat: Don't take offense if either of you scores particularly low. Use the test as a jumping point for discussions to learn more.

INSTRUCTIONS:

Take the quiz. Circle the answers you believe your partner will give. Once you complete the test, pass it to your partner. Whenever there is an answer that is in agreement, mark the X; incorrect answer, mark the O. Add up all the X's and then read the analysis. Switch roles and have your partner check the answer he or she believes you will give. Then mark. Analysis and advice follows.

1. **With an hour of spare time, my partner would like to:**
a. Read.
b. Watch television.
c. Go for a walk.
__X __O

2. **My mate would choose this on the menu:**
a. Pasta or fish
b. Burgers and fries
c. Salad
__X __O

3 The radio is tuned to:

a. Music.

b. News or talk radio.

c. The radio isn't on.

__X __O

4 If a lost kitten was found, my honey would most likely:

a. Keep it until a home was found (posting signs, asking around, etc.).

b. Keep it forever.

c. Feed it, and let it go.

__X __O

5 My lover's politics are mostly to the:

a. Left.

b. Center.

c. Right.

__X __O

6 What's most important to your mate?

a. A creative pursuit

b. Career

c. Family and relationships

__X __O

7 When it comes to the death penalty, my paramour:

a. Is wholly opposed to it.

b. Takes each case on an individual basis.

c. Supports it.

__X __O

8. Which statement best describes your partner's philosophy of life?

a. It's a bowl of cherries.

b. It's a journey.

c. It's just a dream.

___X ___O

9. Which of these rides would your honey like to hitch?

a. Around the track in a sports car

b. Sailing high in a hot air balloon

c. Snowboarding down a powdery mountaintop

___X ___O

10. If my partner ran into an old lover on the street, they would probably:

a. Stop and chat.

b. Go for a drink.

c. Ignore each other or just nod hello and walk on.

___X ___O

Analysis

3 X'S OR LESS

You're still somewhat in the dark about what makes your partner tick. It might mean you're taking it slow, one of you is guarded, or the other isn't paying enough attention. In any case, it's time to earnestly dig deeper.

ADVICE

To help the door open wider:

- Become a good listener. It's not always necessary to respond with your point of view. It's more important to open your heart to what your partner is expressing.

- Reserve judgment. It's human nature to remain guarded if we think someone is going to pounce on our views.
- Simply ask questions. Showing a real interest in someone's feelings and attitudes is the best way to keep the river of communication flowing.

4 TO 7 X'S

You have a pretty good sense of who your partner really is—but there are some areas as yet unexplored or misconstrued. Go over the questions one by one to figure out where there's a gap and then be open to exploring each other's views deeply and without holding back.

ADVICE

To get to know each other better:
- Share more quiet time. Turn down distractions—whether they're the television, the Internet, or your cell phones—and enjoy some open-ended discussions.
- Invite long-time friends and family for dinner. This is a great way to uncover some old secrets.
- Tune in to body language. You're probably missing silent messages so bone up on unspoken cues. Check out this site: http://www.wikihow.com/Read-Body-Language

8 X'S OR MORE

When it comes to your lover, you're tuned in. You have a real knowledge of your mate's values and priorities; even if you don't always see eye-to-eye, your understanding and acceptance is very much appreciated. This kind of intimacy bodes well for an enduring relationship, but there are always things you can do to give it an even bigger boost.

ADVICE

To grow even closer:

- Create a regular date night. Couples who know each other well tend to start taking each other for granted. Keep the flame alive by setting aside one night a week just for romance.
- Go on an adventure. It doesn't have to be three weeks in Marrakech, but you want to build lasting memories together. Consider going on a walking tour of your city, hiking up a mountain, even sharing an exotic meal—one that you'll both remember.
- Celebrate with a handmade gift. Next time a birthday or anniversary rolls around, create a gift that is one of a kind. Personal presents are cherished forever.

"It is not time or opportunity that is to determine intimacy; it is disposition alone. Seven years would be insufficient to make some people acquainted with each other, and seven days are more than enough for others."

—JANE AUSTEN

Exercise

GET TO KNOW THE REAL YOU WITH MIRROR GAZING.
Most of the time we only look at our reflections to see whether or
not we're presentable. If we do pause in front of a mirror, it is often to
criticize ourselves for the way we look rather than merely to observe
what we see. In this mirror-gazing exercise you simply look at yourself
naked (yes!) in a mirror for approximately fifteen minutes, in order to
learn to accept yourself and develop the same loving relationship with
your own body that you wish your lover to have with it. It is important
to regard yourself openly, just as you would look at a friend. You may
find this hard to do initially or may get drawn into criticizing aspects
of yourself you wish were different, but let these thoughts go—and
stay open. Gazing at yourself may also awaken memories or feelings
of sadness or loneliness. Simply register whatever thoughts or feelings
arise. They are all part of the process of getting to know yourself a
little better, and it is only by expressing and accepting your feelings
that you can begin to know and accept who your are.

What Kind of Relationship Do You Really Want?

When you get together with your girlfriends, do you talk about your dream guy? The kind of man who is faithful, romantic, a big-time breadwinner, handsome, stable, *and* makes you burn with desire? Well, except for the last attribute (what girl isn't looking for *that?*) you might be kidding yourself. Psychologists say most of us are drawn to a particular type of man based on issues stemming from our earliest relationships—probably with one of our parents. So even though you may claim to want Mr. Perfect, you might really be on the lookout for Mr. Not-So-Great. Read on and get advice on how to discover what you *really* want.

PART ONE

1. Basically, you're attracted to a certain kind of guy. He's:
a. A hunk—tall, dark, and handsome; real swoon material.
b. A lamb—sweet, sensitive, and sensual; not gorgeous, but always gracious.
c. A bad boy—romantic and riveting; he plays the field and is a high scorer.

2. Let's say you meet a man who lets you know he's not interested in getting serious. Do you think:
a. Maybe that's what he thinks now, but I *know* I can change him.
b. I'll stick with him for a while, but if the situation remains stagnant, I'm splitting.
c. So long. I'm not interested in a frivolous affair.

3. When you were a teenager, what did you love to read?
a. Adventure stories
b. Sappy romances
c. Celebrity biographies

4 And when you surf the net these days, you spend the most time on:

a. Self-improvement pages.

b. Newspapers and political blogs.

c. Celebrity gossip sites.

5 On average, how long do your liaisons last?

a. More than five years

b. More than six months

c. Five weeks, tops

6 Your very best friend introduces you to her new boyfriend, and (horrors!) you instantly feel uncontrollably attracted to him. What do you do?

a. Flirt

b. Fantasize

c. Forget it

7 You feel most comfortable wearing:

a. Lace and velvet.

b. Silk and satin.

c. Pure cotton and cashmere.

8 Which of these statements best describes your feelings about love?

a. It needs to be cultivated if you want it to last.

b. If you keep your heart open, it's always available.

c. It's a wonderful once-in-a-lifetime experience.

SCORING

1. a-5   b-3   c-7

2. a-7   b-5   c-3

3. a-3   b-7   c-5

4. a-7   b-3   c-5
5. a-3   b-5   c-7
6. a-7   b-5   c-3
7. a-5   b-7   c-3
8. a-5   b-7   c-3

PART TWO

Give yourself 3 points for each of the following statements with which you agree.

1   I'll stay interested in a man—even if he's not available.

a. Agree   b. Disagree

2   When I see couples kissing in public, I'm inspired.

a. Agree   b. Disagree

3   Nothing makes me feel more glamorous than falling in love.

a. Agree   b. Disagree

4   The world would be a better place if we were ruled by our hearts, not our heads.

a. Agree   b. Disagree

5   I know practically all the lyrics to the latest love songs.

a. Agree   b. Disagree

Add scores from Part One and Part Two.

Analysis

UP TO 39 POINTS

Sensible and down-to-earth, you know the difference between love and a light-hearted fling. But rather than searching for romance, you let it find you—and when it does, you embrace it with open arms and an open heart. Not one to fool yourself, you never pretend you can change a man. You know better. That's probably why you're likely to fall in love for life. It's not the thrill of romance that makes you feel alive, but the cozy comfort of a calm relationship. The lucky man who chooses you as his partner will share the warm, simple values of family life.

40 TO 55 POINTS

You try hard to distinguish between innocent flirtation and real-life romance, but unfortunately, you sometimes confuse love with lust. You're optimistic and trusting by nature and perhaps that's why you fall for more lines than Little Red Riding Hood. Some men really are the big, bad wolf, though you might pretend otherwise. ('Fess up: you sometimes enjoy being fooled!) Though you really believe you're looking for the love of a lifetime, a part of you still wants drama more than a gold ring. You're not ready to settle down right now—so accept it and just enjoy yourself.

56 POINTS OR MORE

No two ways about it, you would rather fall in love than be in love. You're addicted to the thrill of the new and still mysterious romance. Once a relationship starts to grow, you get bored and begin the hunt all over again. In actuality, commitment and security are scaring you away. That's why you must have romance in your life, or you're likely to feel empty, worthless, and at odds. It may be a hard lesson to learn, but it's probably low self-esteem that keeps you addicted to love. You need to build inner confidence. Start today by making a list of your strengths and keep it growing. Before long you'll start a new chapter in your life.

Exercises

HOW TO BE HONEST ABOUT WHAT YOU REALLY WANT.

Marilyn Graman, author of *There is No Prince and Other Truths Your Mother Never Told You,* says, "Finding the partner who will make you happy is one of the most important things in life. Why leave it up to chance or fate?"

Her suggestion is to make a list of what she calls the six "musts":

- Do I want to be married?
- Do I want to have children?
- Do I want someone who shares my religion?
- Do I want someone with a certain amount of financial stability?
- Do I want someone who lives where I live now?
- Do I want someone who will devote a lot of time to me? Or do I want more independence?

Next, move on to what Graman calls the ten "very importants."
These may not be deal breakers but still fall into the area of priorities. Some questions you could ask are:

- Do I want someone who has been married before?
- Has children?
- Owns his home?
- Likes to travel?
- Is a reader?
- Is a sports fan?
- Has a college degree?
- Is well-groomed?

Then, move onto the six "must nots." For example, he:

- Must not be a substance abuser.
- Must not cheat.
- Must not have an anger issue.
- Must not have a lot of debt.
- Must not be a control freak.
- Must not be needy.

After you sort through your honest, no-holds-barred lists, keep them handy. If you're involved in a relationship now, ask yourself, "Am I really with the kind of man I want to be with?" If you're on the lookout, refer to your list. It's easy to kid ourselves, but the consequences aren't so much fun. It's best to look at what we want with open and honest eyes. Why fool yourself?

"If you want to make your dreams come true, the first thing you have to do is wake up."

—J.M. POWER

What's Your Fighting Style? Take a Peek in Your Closet to Find Out!

Getting into arguments is a natural dynamic of relationships. In fact, the ability to fight is a predictor of a couple's success—and what matters most is not what you fight about but *how* you do it. Do you take the gloves off before you pull a punch? Or do you go right for the jugular? You may think you know how you work out your anger, but research shows we're pretty clueless when it comes to the way we express displeasure. And here's even more of a shocker: Social scientists have discovered that our *closets* reveals hidden secrets about our fighting style. It's true! "What you choose to wear, keep, or give away, and how you hang your clothes, all reveal whether you react directly and spontaneously, or are a mistress of passive aggressive behavior," says Linda Koopersmith, co-host of Style Network's *Clean House* and author of *The Beverly Hills Organizer's Home Organizing Bible*. To discover what your closet is saying about your fighting style, take this quiz.

1   **When scanning your closet, which colors dominate?**
a. Brights
b. Neutrals

2   **Is yours a closet for all seasons?**
a. Yes. Wool blazers and sundresses share the same rod.
b. No. My spring and summer clothes are stored away.

3   **Most of my blouses are on hangers made of:**
a. Wire.
b. Plastic or wood.

4 If the button popped off slacks you wanted to wear, you would be more likely to:

a. Put them back in your closet and sew the button back on later.

b. Take out your sewing kit and mend it right away.

5 The clothes in your closet are:

a. Packed like sardines.

b. Spaced out like tines on a fork.

6 You usually arrange your wardrobe by:

a. Favorites—the outfits you like best are the easiest to reach.

b. Color, style, or season.

7 On the inside of your closet door, you'd prefer to hang a:

a. Couple of sturdy hooks for grab-and-go accessories.

b. A full-length mirror.

8 When's the last time you cleared your closet of outdated/ill-fitting items?

a. Can't remember the last time

b. Last season

9 In general, do you take more than five minutes to browse through your closet and think about what you're going to wear?

a. Rarely

b. Usually

10 When your special clothes come back from the dry cleaner, you usually:

a. Hang them in the closet.

b. Remove the plastic so they can "breathe" before putting them away.

11 You keep your shoes:

a. On the floor.

b. In a shoe bag or on a shoe tree.

12 Most of your skirts:

a. Join one another on the same multi-item hanger.

b. Hang alone.

Analysis

MOSTLY A'S
YOU ACT FIRST, THINK LATER.

Fashionable, energetic, and extremely personable, you're usually too busy enjoying the moment to worry about minor details like lining up your shoes, tacking up a loose hem, or hanging your blouses according to color. "Your playful, usually forgiving nature—and haphazard closet habits—means you live in the moment rather than project into the future," says Koopersmith. "It also means your fighting style is spontaneous and fiery." You may lash out in an instant but a minute later, all is forgiven. Hold on! Your partner might not feel the same way. Sometimes you say things in a fit of pique, which are better left unspoken. You may also blow problems out of proportion. Or worse, play the blame game. Well, there's a better way to fight; here are a few suggestions:

ADVICE

- Calm down and listen to each other *fully* while you fight. This includes watching body language.
- Look at each other while you speak.
- Don't interrupt during your fight.
- Try to use "I" sentences instead of "You" sentences.
- Avoid blaming and making accusations.

- If the two of you are not extremely angry, try to hold hands while arguing.
- Do not yell. Do not scream. Do not talk in a threatening tone.

MOSTLY B'S
YOU THINK FIRST AND ACT LATER.

Like your closet, you're neat, efficient, well-organized, and a pro at planning ahead and considering all options before making any moves. "Your meticulously prepared day means you get a lot accomplished and friends and family can rely on responsible-you to help out," says Koopersmith. "But it also means you're the queen at stuffing problems, putting off your grievances, and letting problems fester and grow out of proportion because you haven't given them air to breathe." It's better to give voice to what's bothering you before your anger gains strength and ends up leaking out in crazy ways. Try this:

ADVICE
- If you are angry about something, talk about it within forty-eight hours.
- Know what the issue is. Name it and stick to the subject.
- Don't bring up past history.
- Be careful how you use humor. Laughter is good, but teasing can be misinterpreted and hurtful.
- Don't use the words "never" and "always" in your statements to each other.
- Even though it may be hard to forgive your partner, not forgiving can cause more harm, both emotionally and physically, to yourself and to your relationship.
- Holding a grudge is letting someone else live in your head rent-free.

Exercise

Think about a situation recently where you felt angry. Picture the situation in your mind and remember what you were feeling and thinking. How did your body feel at the time? Can you feel any of those body signals right now? List four body signals you get when you are feeling angry:

1. _____

2. _____

3. _____

4. _____

Note: Usually after our body begins to feel anger signals we begin to act angry. This often happens before we actually realize that we are feeling angry.

"For every minute you're angry you lose sixty seconds of happiness."

—RALPH WALDO EMERSON

How Do You Perceive Your Partner's Personality?

There's something to the expression "Love is blind." When we're in love, our brains are manufacturing a feel-good brain chemical called oxytocin. Naturally high, we believe what we perceive is our lover's true nature. But experts report we tend to view our partners as archetypes (ideal examples), and our impression is formed through the lens of our own experiences—not necessarily what's happening in the here and now. Yet, for a healthy, long-lasting relationship, it's best to keep it real. It's the only way your relationship can unfold and develop. This test will help you see what you're focusing on. Travis Bradberry, PhD, author of *The Emotional Intelligence Quick Book,* says, "By looking at your partner's reaction to situations, you'll discover his most impressive quality and learn how it affects you—and your relationship."

1 Of these, the character trait you think is his strongest is:

a. Friendliness.

b. Trustworthiness.

c. Decisiveness.

2 You'd describe his handshake as:

a. Somewhat firm.

b. Soft and warm.

c. Strong.

3 He's most likely to begin a call with a friend by saying something like:

a. I was just thinking about you.

b. What have you been up to?

c. I can't wait to tell you . . .

4 If the person behind you at the movies started talking a lot, your guy would:

a. Ask the person to be quiet in a pleasant voice.

b. Turn around to give the person a look.

c. Face the screen but whisper, "Shhhh!"

5 If your man was around a toddler who wouldn't share and grabbed a toy from another little one, he would most likely:

a. Tell him he needs to share and have him give the toy back.

b. Ask him if there's another toy he'd like to share.

c. Return the toy to the other child himself.

6 Who initiates lovemaking more?

a. I'm not sure.

b. I do.

c. He does.

7 **If a co-worker took credit for his ideas, he'd probably:**

a. Take the co-worker aside and privately suggest that he or she corrects the error.

b. Let it go—this time.

c. Politely correct his co-worker immediately in front of whoever was listening.

Analysis

MOSTLY A'S
HIS MOST IMPRESSIVE QUALITY
IS HIS INCOMPARABLE SOCIAL SKILL.

No matter the situation or the person he's dealing with, he usually intuitively knows what to say or do. That's because he recognizes that others want to feel important and all it takes is some positive feedback. People appreciate this. "His outgoing nature rallies people to him," says Bradberry.

ADVICE

It's common for couples to let one person be the social butterfly while the other one becomes more passive. But there's room for two to be in the limelight. Try this:

· Make a list of actions or goals you want to reach and then give yourself a deadline to achieve them. When you take actions step-by-step, you'll be less likely to feel like a shrinking violet.

· Try saying yes instead of no. Your first reaction may be to turn down a challenge but think it over again. Exploring different options can actually expand your ability to shine.

· Schedule in double dates and share the social scene. Practice using your charisma to engage friends in conversation.

MOSTLY B'S
HIS MOST IMPRESSIVE QUALITY
IS HIS ABILITY TO READ OTHERS.

From the shift in his body language to the tone of his voice, your guy has no trouble reading other people. His ability to put himself in others' shoes drives this trait. And he's a good listener, too. "When you listen to what's on a person's mind, barriers are broken—and they'll be receptive to what you say," says Bradberry.

ADVICE

Since your guy is the master at communication, you've let your diplomatic skills go to seed. Here's how to replenish them:

- Delegate. Allow others who have expertise to carry some of the load. If it makes you uncomfortable to let someone else share responsibility, it's okay to check in once in a while.
- Open your palms. Surprisingly, a study shows this simple gesture of letting go actually helps release the impulse to take over situations.
- Eat foods rich in B6, which will help to keep your nervous system steady during up and down times: spinach, tuna, walnuts, white meat chicken and turkey, bananas, and raisins are all good choices.

MOSTLY C'S
HIS MOST IMPRESSIVE QUALITY IS HIS INDEPENDENCE.

Whenever he enters a room, his confidence comes through just by his posture and the way he walks. "When you have confidence, people feel sure about you and want to follow your lead," says Bradberry. His high self-esteem and take-charge qualities means he's capable of setting forth a plan, but he also knows how to compromise when it's necessary.

ADVICE

This means you often step aside and let him take over. To make sure you're also meeting your potential:

- Set daily goals. The longer your list, the less you're likely to accomplish, so keep it to a maximum of five things.
- Learn to take a breather and relax. Even though he's calm and relaxed about being in the driver's seat, you tense up if it's your turn. Take a deep breath and tell yourself, "I can do this!"
- Shut down distractions and limit multitasking. Studies show when you don't give full attention to a primary task you'll make 30 percent more mistakes and can spend up to 20 percent more time correcting them.
- Do tai chi, yoga, or meditation exercises. You have the perfect personality for these proven confidence-boosting practices. Plus, each of them can help you find your strong center.

"Love is ¾ dream and ¼ reality.
Problems usually arise when you fall in
love with the dream and not the reality.
But, yet you find true love when you
fall in love with both."

—UNKNOWN

Exercise

FIND OUT IF HE'S TELLING THE TRUTH.

According to Gary Pearlman, author of the article "How to Spot a Liar", there are concrete ways to find out if your guy is telling the truth. Pay attention to these cues:

Liars tend to move their arms, hands, and fingers less and blink less than people telling the truth do. Liars usually do not use their hands much, and they often fold their arms together in front of them or position items such as books, cups, or other things between themselves and the person asking the questions.

Liars' voices can become more tense or high-pitched. The extra effort needed to remember what they've already said and to keep their stories consistent may cause liars to restrain their movements and fill their speech with pauses. People shading the truth tend to make fewer speech errors than truth tellers do, and they rarely backtrack to fill in forgotten or incorrect details. .

People who lie tend to favor bold facts. Liars tend to string together very simple actions and avoid details.

Sadness is very hard to fake. When someone is genuinely sad, the forehead wrinkles with grief and the inner corners of the eyebrows are pulled up. By contrast, the lowering of the eyebrows associated with an angry scowl can be faked by almost everybody. If someone says they are sad and the inner corners of their eyebrows don't go up, they are likely faking it.

People who are uncomfortable or lying often repeat the question you ask them.

When we smile genuinely we move more than just our mouth, the *orbicularis oculi,* the muscle around the eye that gives us "crow's-feet," also moves. Liars tend to just move their mouths. It takes only two muscles, the *zygomaticus* major muscles that extend from the cheekbones to the corners of the lips to produce a grin.

Liars may also feel fear and guilt or delight at fooling people. Such emotions can trigger a change in facial expression so brief that most observers never notice. These split-second "micro-expressions" are emotional clues as important as gestures, voice, and speech patterns in uncovering deceitfulness.

A liar's speech pattern changes. Liars may mispronounce words, mumble, and take longer pauses between a question and a response than honest people. This happens because the liar is not sure where they're going with the lie or might be having trouble following through with the lie.

Looking down while talking may indicate someone is embarrassed or does not know, looking to their right (your left) would indicate that they are constructing or making something up.

How Well Do You Know Your Partner?

Way back in the seventies there was a popular television quiz show called *The Newlywed Game*, where contestants would try and guess their partners' preferences. Winners got a great vacation, a living room set, or a year's supply of frozen dinners. Well, this quiz is just like it—without the cameras and competition—and the only prize you get is satisfaction! Even better: you take it privately—just the two of you. If you keep your answers honest, you'll not only discover just how much you really know about each other, but how much more there's still to learn. Remember: A relationship unfolds like a flower, so even if you miss the mark, given time, more will open and be revealed.

INSTRUCTIONS:

Take the quiz. Circle the answers you believe are correct. Once the test is completed, pass it to your partner. Whenever there is an answer that is correct, mark the X; incorrect answer, mark the O. Add up all X's to read the analysis. Switch roles. Analysis and advice follows.

1   **Favorite flavor:**

a. Sweet

b. Savory

c. Spicy

__X __O

2   **Pet preference:**

a. Dog

b. Cat

c. Bird or fish

__X __O

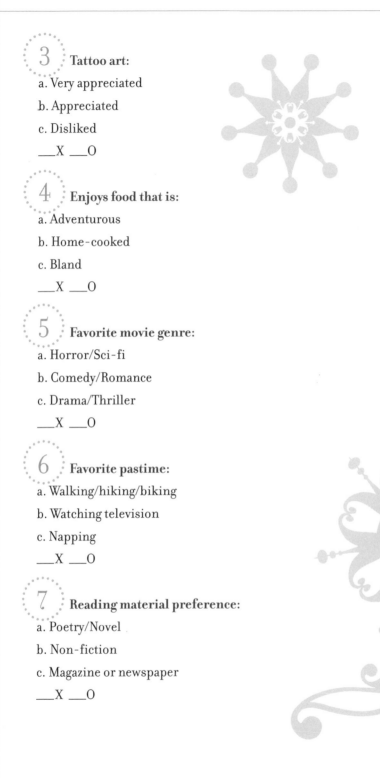

3 Tattoo art:

a. Very appreciated

b. Appreciated

c. Disliked

__X __O

4 Enjoys food that is:

a. Adventurous

b. Home-cooked

c. Bland

__X __O

5 Favorite movie genre:

a. Horror/Sci-fi

b. Comedy/Romance

c. Drama/Thriller

__X __O

6 Favorite pastime:

a. Walking/hiking/biking

b. Watching television

c. Napping

__X __O

7 Reading material preference:

a. Poetry/Novel

b. Non-fiction

c. Magazine or newspaper

__X __O

8 **Remembers his dreams:**

a. Regularly

b. Sometimes

c. Rarely or never

___X ___O

9 **Lost? He would prefer to:**

a. Ask someone on the street or at a gas station.

b. Look at a map.

c. Check back to Google maps.

___X ___O

10 **Best vacation spot:**

a. Edgy foreign city

b. Rustic country cabin

c. Ultra-relaxing beach holiday or spa

___X ___O

11 **Deals with problems by:**

a. Talking them over

b. Working them out alone

c. With avoidance

___X ___O

12 **Happiest when:**

a. Socializing

b. Engaging in a physical activity

c. Relaxing alone

___X ___O

Analysis

BETWEEN 9 AND 12 X'S
YOU'VE GOT HIS NUMBER.

Whether you've been seeing each other for a long time or just a short while, you have a good sense of your partner—at least when it comes to this quiz. But here's the snag: Familiarity doesn't necessarily breed contempt as the old adage goes—but it often does create a level of complacency. Don't take your lover for granted.

ADVICE

- Ask questions. Even though you may believe you can read his mind (and often you can) it's best to be direct.
- Write a love letter and describe every reason why you're meant to be together.
- Dress each other. You undress each other without a second thought—but try doing it in reverse for a terrific intimacy builder.

BETWEEN 8 AND 5 X'S
YOU USUALLY HAVE HIM PEGGED.

For the most part, you know what makes his world go 'round, but there are still some loose spokes in the wheel. These are the kinds of things that can create bumps in the road, so you want to be more attentive to your partner's true preferences. To really know your mate, follow these suggestions for better communication:

ADVICE

- Don't make assumptions. Try to approach each situation with a blank slate.
- Before speaking be sure that he's finished. You do this by slowing down your mind and not anticipating an answer.
- Reserve judgment during the conversation and beyond. If you keep an open mind, you'll reap the benefit of open-ended conversations.

4 X'S OR LESS
YOU'RE MISSING THE POINT.

You say you love each other but there are still some big intimacy gaps. It's true that not everyone is able to open up and share their deepest thoughts—and it's not always necessary. But it *is* crucial to "get" the keys to your partner's happiness. Without a feeling of connectedness, doubts and dissatisfaction start to emerge and can eventually lead to serious problems. You need to know each other's priorities and values as well as the day-to-day pleasures. Here are a few ways you can build true intimacy:

ADVICE

- Spend time alone together every day. Set aside at least half an hour daily and begin to talk from the place of your authentic selves. As you do so, you'll begin to experience being more vulnerable with each other.
- Be consciously silent in each other's company. This nourishes a soul connection.
- Deal with relationship issues as soon as they arise. Don't drag out issues by ignoring or denying them. This contributes to the great divide.

"My friends tell me I have an intimacy problem, but they don't really know me."

—GARRY SHANDLING

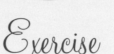

MEDITATE TOGETHER

Meditation has profound effects on our well-being and can open a door to self-knowledge as well as deepen our love for others. Doing it as a couple doubles its benefits. But it doesn't have to be a complicated process. Advanced meditators may prefer to sit on a cushion in a lotus or half-lotus position and focus on their breathing or on a particular mantra. For beginners, follow these basic steps together:

- Sit in a quiet, comfortable place on a straight-back chair or floor cushion. Relax your muscles, but do not lie down.
- Select a syllable, phrase, or word, such as "one," "love," or "om."
- Close your eyes and follow the rhythm of your breathing, relaxing a little more with each breath. You'll be surprised at how quickly your breathing will soon synchronize.
- Repeat your chosen word as you breathe in and out. If your mind wanders, don't quit. Just let your thoughts go, and refocus by repeating your chosen word.
- Continue for ten to twenty minutes—agree on the amount of time beforehand—and stick to it.
- When you're both finished, sit quietly for a minute or two together. Then open your eyes and enjoy a long, deeply satisfying hug.

What's His Fighting Strength?

My pet peeve when it comes to a guy's fighting strength is the moping man. For me, nothing is worse than the silent treatment. But you might not agree. It doesn't really matter what your personal preference is; it's more important to be able to identify the way your guy voices his displeasure and be able to respond so he feels understood. What? You say you *never fight*? Think again: No two people in the world, no matter how made for each other they feel, will ever agree about *everything* at all times. What's more, it's good to let off steam. Jill Spiegel, author of *The Pocket Pep Talk*, says, "Couples who have healthy fights develop a kind of efficacy that makes the relationship stronger as time goes on." In recognition of the usefulness of arguing—find out what kind of fighter you've fallen for!

1   **When packing for a trip, he usually:**

a. Gives himself a small but comfortable margin of time to spare.

b. Throws things into the suitcase at the last minute.

c. Packs carefully and well in advance.

2   **The last time he was stuck in traffic, he:**

a. Tuned in to music and just kept inching his way along.

b. Switched lanes to get ahead.

c. Turned on the traffic report to get an idea of the delay.

3   **When he makes a mistake, does he usually react by saying:**

a. "Let me try again."

b. "What can I learn from this?"

c. "How can I do it differently next time?"

4 During the evening hours, he prefers to:

a. Curl up in front of the TV set.

b. Catch up on whatever needs to be done.

c. Make up tomorrow's schedule.

5 What was his best subject in high school?

a. English or history

b. Art or music

c. Math or science

6 If a cocktail he was planning to serve to guests didn't come out exactly as expected, he would most likely:

a. Serve it anyway.

b. Doctor it up—fast!

c. Switch to an entirely different drink.

7 He prefers to:

a. Watch sports.

b. Play sports.

c. Ignore sports.

8 When it comes to watching television, he usually:

a. Goes with his favorites.

b. Channel surfs.

c. Checks the listings in advance.

9 Would he consult a feng shui expert before decorating his apartment?

a. If it matched his decorating taste.

b. Absolutely.

c. Are you kidding? No way!

10 If the forecast was for bright skies, but there were sudden looming clouds just as he was about to go for a hike, he would most likely:

a. Take his chances and just leave.

b. Reschedule.

c. Grab rain gear and go.

Analysis

MOSTLY A'S
HIS FIGHTING STRENGTH IS RESILIENCY.

He bounces right back because he knows arguing is just part of the process—a stepping-stone toward intimacy. "He's deeply positive, optimistic, and self-confident," says Jill Spiegel. "It's why he can keep walking forward no matter what difficulties you both encounter." In fact, studies show resiliency is the number one trait of folks who rank highest on the scale of emotional intelligence—a prime predictor of relationship success.

MOSTLY B'S
HIS FIGHTING STRENGTH IS FLEXIBILITY.

Outstanding at finding alternative routes to compromise, he's super adaptable, can change directions easily, and stays open-minded to a wide range of possibilities. "Surveys show folks who are flexible are easy to get along with because they don't hold too firmly to only one way of doing things," says Spiegel. "They consider difficulty a challenge—not a defeat!" Spontaneous, able to think on his feet, and naturally creative—he's pretty easy going. And since he can bend easily, even when there's a sudden surprise and plans fall apart, he remains calm, steady, and centered.

MOSTLY C'S
HIS FIGHTING STRENGTH COMES
FROM A STRONG SENSE OF REASON.

As a strategic thinker, he can analyze any situation and think through problems quickly because he's able to look at both the big picture and small details all at once. "He also knows how to evaluate information," says Spiegel. "He gathers advice and researches the facts, but ultimately uses his own sense of practical reasoning to come to the right conclusion." As a man who knows how to stand back *and* look ahead, he's usually fully prepared, which means whatever life hands over he's ready to take it on!

Advice

Regardless of fighting strengths or styles, whenever you need to discuss something really heavy that's likely to bring up disagreements, it's best to plan for it.

- Decide when. Identify a good time for your discussion. Avoid times when either of you are tired, children may be listening, or stress may be looming. If it is a time when you are both relaxed, it is likely to work better.
- Decide where. Find a neutral location for your discussion. Avoid discussions in your bed or in locations where you are likely to be interrupted.
- Decide what. Agree on the topic or the problem for discussion beforehand.

Exercise

Arguing can make anyone tense even if your guy's fighting style is reasonable. Experts suggest one of the best ways to relieve stress and tension is with Progressive Muscle Relaxation or PMR. Here's how to do it:

- Lie down or sit comfortably in a chair.
- Begin by tensing all the muscles in your face, including your jaw and eyes. Hold it tight for the count of ten while inhaling.
- Exhale and release.
- Next, move on down your body from your neck muscles, arms, torso, groin, legs, to your feet. With each muscle group, tense, inhale, then exhale, and release.

"I don't mind arguing with myself.
It's when I lose that it bothers me."

—RICHARD POWERS

How Committed Is Your Partner?

Whether you're married or dating, the effort your partner puts into the relationship sends out a clear signal. It's either flashing: a) *really committed to making things work*, b) *not exactly sure*, or c) *sabotaging our future together*. And don't think just because you've been a couple for a decade, or even two, that your relationship is immune to erosion. Even long-term relationships can get weak in the commitment department. *Hello?* Has he forgotten your anniversary? Take this quiz to get insight into whether your man is really taking solid steps toward moving your relationship into the future—or if he's backing off.

1. **You're feeling sad. He is:**
a. Right there with you asking questions to find out how he can help.
b. Calling a few times during the day just to check in.
c. Busy with his problems.

2. **He spends time with his friends:**
a. Every now and then.
b. Once a week.
c. Every single chance he gets.

3. **When Valentine's Day rolls around, he's:**
a. Gotten a gift that makes your heart melt.
b. Offering the standard chocolate, flowers, or card.
c. Forgotten.

4. **How often does he bring you coffee or tea?**
a. Frequently
b. Rarely
c. Never

5 If you were feeling under the weather, he would most likely:

a. Make chicken soup.

b. Ask what he could do to help you feel better.

c. Be gone. He's a bit germ phobic.

6 Have you met his family and friends?

a. Of course.

b. Most of them.

c. Only by accident, if we bump into someone on the street.

7 When you're feeling overwhelmed with the day, he:

a. Helps out either cooking or cleaning or picking up groceries.

b. Asks what he can do.

c. Sits in front of the television so he won't get in your way.

8 How often does he tell you that he loves you?

a. All the time

b. At least once a day

c. On a very rare occasion—and not lately

9 Which of these statements best describes how up-to-the-minute he is on your life?

a. He's on the same page.

b. He's somewhere in the chapter.

c. He never opens the book.

10 When you fight, he usually:

a. Listens to your side.

b. Walks away to avoid disagreement.

c. Stands his ground no matter what.

Analysis

MOSTLY A'S
HE'S REALLY COMMITTED TO MAKING THINGS WORK.

There's not another person on earth with whom he'd rather spend his life. Your partner turns to you in good times and bad, and you do the same. While other couples may drift apart after years together, each day brings the two of you closer. One of your secrets to relationship success is that you both know how to communicate effectively. You each listen and lend support when needed—and you also know when to respect the other's need for a certain amount of privacy. With this perfect balance, it's not surprising he's committed to you 100 percent. It's all good, but it can get better. How? Work on keeping your romance alive.

ADVICE
- Make time for sexual contact. If your schedules are packed, plan for it.
- Have a relaxing bath, get out a candle, and surprise him by wearing something new and sexy. Even if he's 100 percent committed, don't go to bed wearing a flannel gown *every* night!

MOSTLY B'S
HE'S NOT EXACTLY SURE.

You've both traveled on some bumpy roads and he occasionally may think the grass is greener on the other side—and that's why he's not quite positive about moving forward. But his biggest problem isn't dissatisfaction with you. It's his inability to express how he feels. Instead of speaking out, he clams up, and the silence and frustration between you builds. Strive for openness and trust. Since you both want to be committed to each other, it requires conscientious effort to make it work.

ADVICE

- Remember you're a team. A relationship isn't about winning; it's about pulling together in the same direction. Stop for a moment and look honestly at yourself. Do you need to win every argument or be right about some insignificant disagreement?
- Shut off electronic distractions and set aside time to talk each day.
- Be generous with casual physical contact like a hug or a kiss hello, or brush against him as you walk by.

MOSTLY C'S

HE'S SABOTAGING THE FUTURE.

It's probably no surprise to you that your man isn't exactly making a commitment. Yes, your relationship does have its problems, but most relationships can be saved. If you both want to make the effort to continue, consult a counselor or your clergy. And take time to devote to stress-free romantic evenings or a weekend together. Your love is still there. It just needs rekindling.

ADVICE

- Be deliberate in building intimacy. Start small by sharing a TV program and snuggling beside him.
- Share your thoughts. Even if you think he's not listening, let him know how you're feeling—and then ask his advice.
- Make daily contact when you're not together either through e-mail, text, or a phone call.
- Be willing to let go. If all your overtures lead to a closed door, walk away.

Exercise

WATCH THE SUNSET TOGETHER.

Gaze upon a sunset and, research shows, you'll feel closer in just a few brilliant minutes! That's because watching the sunset promotes the same benefits as ten minutes of meditation. It relaxes muscle tension, reduces blood pressure, and eliminates worries and irritability. What a beautiful and peaceful way to end your day together.

"Go confidently in the direction of your dreams.
Live the life you imagined."

—HENRY DAVID THOREAU

What Are Your Partner's Goals in a Relationship?

Forget the serenades by moonlight or rose-petal-strewn sheets—although both would be nice! If you want your relationship to thrive you'd be advised to come up with a joint mission statement. A survey of six hundred couples found that pursuing common goals with the same intensity is the key to lasting love. "The problem is that different goals and priorities create arguments and conflict," explains Warwick Hosking, PhD, the researcher who conducted the study. "Opposites attract" is really a fallacy and only romantic folklore. The adage that makes more sense is: "Birds of a feather flock together." Take this test to discover where your partner puts his focus and whether it's in sync with yours.

1 **Do you consider your partner a risk taker?**
a. Not really
b. Sometimes
c. Absolutely

2 **How does he react when meeting new people?**
a. A little uncomfortable at first
b. Enjoys it
c. Is always at ease and tries to learn from the interaction

3 **Given a choice, would he take a job which:**
a. Lets him work from home.
b. Gives him a chance to express himself.
c. Includes lots of travel.

4 **He would describe his main career objective as:**
a. Providing income for daily needs.
b. Making a difference in the world.
c. Doing something he enjoys and can be recognized for.

5 Other than the computer, what item on his desk does he glance at most often?

a. A framed picture of you, his family, or his pet

b. A daily appointment book

c. A can-do affirmation

6 If he wanted a stress-busting vacation, would he book a:

a. Secluded resort.

b. Disney vacation.

c. Luxury spa.

7 Where would he most likely place a bet?

a. On a sports game

b. At the poker table

c. With a scratch-off lottery ticket

8 If he had a break, which of these classic adventure movies would he watch?

a. *Indiana Jones*

b. *Star Wars*

c. *Back to the Future*

9 If he were in the mood for a leisurely drive, where would he head?

a. Down a country road

b. Around town

c. To the mall

10 If he came into a large inheritance, he would most likely:

a. Put it in the bank.

b. Invest in a low-risk stock.

c. Spend a chunk on "toys."

Analysis

MOSTLY A'S
HE'S AFRAID TO SET GOALS.

Psychologists call your man "risk aversive"—meaning he's most comfortable when he can see exactly what's on the road ahead of him. Unfortunately, even though this means he's pretty easy going, he's also usually standing still—or not going very far. It affects his ability to set goals in your relationship as well as in other areas of his life. This may create a conflict for you since you're more of a high-achiever and tend to set goals for yourself. What can you do to help him let go a little more?

ADVICE

- The next time an opportunity presents itself and he's afraid to go for it, tell him to ask himself: What's the worst thing that could happen if it doesn't work out? To be involved in a relationship—or to set any goals—you have to accept that nothing in life is certain.
- Teach him to breathe. Risk-aversive types are usually tense. Next time he's faced with a challenge tell him to take ten deep breaths.
- Be open to talking it over. He may see the world differently than you do, but he's a good listener. Try to stay calm while trying to discuss how you see your future with him.

MOSTLY B'S
HIS GOALS ARE PRACTICAL.

Your man always looks before he leaps. Ahead of any kind of decision, whether it's financial or romantic, he weighs the pros and cons carefully. That's usually the sign of someone who has his priorities in order, isn't a huge risk taker, and can be trusted to toe the line and remain a true-blue partner and trusted ally. But sometimes thinking for too long or being too careful means he misses the boat on life's golden opportunities. Remember the adage: "He who hesitates is lost." You can help him be more adventuresome (like you) by:

ADVICE

- Encouraging him to trust his instincts! Research shows that with conscientious types like him, his hunches are right 90 percent of the time.
- Helping him take risks. Not the kind that jeopardize your relationship! Think sky-diving or rollerblading.
- Assuring him that even if he makes a mistake—and takes a risk that doesn't pay off—you'll still stand by him.

MOSTLY C'S

HE SETS HIS GOALS HIGH.

Okay. Your man is fearless and this sense of "anything is possible" has led to some terrific twists of fate. But you probably also want to be sure that he'll always be there for you and is willing to make compromises if you don't exactly agree with the way he sees the world. To do this:

ADVICE

- Suggest he sleep on it before making any major changes.
- Ask him to talk over decisions with those who will be affected by them—that means you!
- Encourage him to follow his dreams—but make sure he also creates a Plan B.

"Shoot for the moon. Even if you miss, you'll land among the stars."

—LES BROWN

 Exercise

Shared goals and visions of the future help couples stay together and focus on what is most important. It is the piece of a relationship that many of us have either forgotten or refuse to look at. Having a goal in a relationship is like a tennis player who focuses on the ball; nothing around him really matters. To find out if your goals match, make a list of *your* ten goals in order of importance. Ask him to do the same. See if they match—or whether you're playing on different courts.

	YOURS	HIS
1.	_____	_____
2.	_____	_____
3.	_____	_____
4.	_____	_____
5.	_____	_____
6.	_____	_____
7.	_____	_____
8.	_____	_____
9.	_____	_____
10.	_____	_____

FACTOID

Studies show men are activity-oriented. So the next time you want your man to really tune in, choose a time and place when he's most relaxed. The best times might be while walking or driving or otherwise engaged in a simple activity.

Chapter Three:
Know Your Relationship

What's Your C.Q.—Compatibility Quotient?

"When people say, 'We're *inc*ompatible,' that usually means, 'We don't get along very well,'" says Ted Huston, PhD, psychology professor at the University of Texas who runs the PAIR project—a longitudinal study of married couples. "People overemphasize the effect of personality or values and they underemphasize the extent to which easy, congenial temperaments aid relationships." Yet, few would argue that most of us *want* someone who is not only great in bed, but can share our laughter, be our best friend, *and* who will keep our secrets, love our families, and enjoy the same adventures. In other words, we want to mesh with our man and yes, be compatible. But it's not as simple as it sounds. Compatibility doesn't necessarily hinge completely on a personal inventory of traits. Nor is it something you automatically have. It's something you make. It's a process—one that you negotiate as you go along, again and again. It's a disposition, an attitude, a willingness to work. Take this compatibility test and discover where you are at as a couple and what you can do to grow together.

1 Are you on the same sleep and wake-up schedules?
   Yes No

2 Do you like the same kinds of music?
   Yes No

3 Do you choose to relax in the same way?
   Yes No

4 Would you both enjoy the same television shows/movies?
   Yes No

5 When it comes to money, are you both on the same save or spend page?
   Yes No

6 Do you like each other's families?
   Yes No

7 When decorating a room, do you share the same taste?
   Yes No

8 Do you like the way he smells?
   Yes No

9 Are you into his sense of style?
   Yes No

10 Do you argue in the same way?
    Yes No

11 Do you think he respects you?

Yes No

12 Do you respect him?

Yes No

13 Would you share a dark secret with him?

Yes No

14 Has he opened up and shared something deep with you?

Yes No

15 Do you both want (or not want) children?

Yes No

16 Would you choose to go on the same kind of vacation?

Yes No

17 Do you like each other's friends?

Yes No

18 Do you like each other's fashion flavor?

Yes No

19 Do you enjoy the same kinds of physical activities?

Yes No

20 Would you rather make love to him than anyone else?

Yes No

21 Do you share the same political perspective?

Yes No

22 Do you view religion in a similar way?

Yes No

23 Are your life goals compatible?

Yes No

24 Can you trust him to do the right thing?

Yes No

25 Do you find the same kinds of jokes funny?

Yes No

Analysis

BETWEEN 18 AND 25 YESES
YOU'RE TOTALLY COMPATIBLE.

You scored extremely high on the compatibility scale because you not only read your guy like a book—you're on the same page. When he speaks you can finish his sentence because you're thinking the same thought. You almost *anticipate* his needs, wants, hopes, and dreams because they're yours, too. More importantly, you let your man know you don't want to make him into somebody else—you accept and love him 100 percent exactly for who he is. For obvious reasons, it's easy to do. Think about a mirror. Yes, you're his reflection—and he's yours! So, what could possibly improve your relationship? The simple truth is that sometimes when everything goes along like salt through a shaker, the relationship gets boring. Spice it up by:

ADVICE

- Forgetting about the bed. Use the kitchen counter, the dining room table, the top of the dryer, or a blanket on the floor.
- Surprising him in the shower. You'll save the planet and time if you add shampooing to the event.
- Sharing a fantasy. Not only is curiosity sexy, it also has the power to shift your relationship.

BETWEEN 10 AND 17 YESES
YOU'VE GOT GREAT INSTINCTS.

Okay, so you may not match every single criterion in the compatibility test and thus, you may not read him perfectly all of the time, but since you follow your instincts about how to handle situations (even the sticky ones) in your relationship, you're usually on target. What's more, even though you don't have a particular strategy, you can intuit when to back down and when to stand your ground. In fact, you possess the most important skill when it comes to compatibility: compromise! Plus, you can always sense when he needs a hug—or some quiet time by himself. Most of the time, your love feels absolutely right. However, when it's a little edgy:

ADVICE

- Ask what's going on. During those rare times when you don't have a clue, be direct. Research into happy relationships shows that communication is more important than compatibility.
- Take a break. Since you're both hard workers, even a day trip to the country is likely to allow more time and space to exchange thoughts.
- Make a list of all your assumptions. Then check it out with him. You might be surprised at where you're off base.

9 OR FEWER YESES
YOU FOLLOW YOUR OWN HEART.

Does it really matter if you're compatible if you're madly in love? Well, yes and no. A real romantic, you're a sentimental and loving soul who may not share her guy's views but always gives 100 percent in trying to make him happy. Sound familiar? Well, this works for a while, but it could lead to resentment. Being a martyr isn't a healthy way to sustain a relationship. Plus, as a full-fledged nurturer who makes her man's interests a priority, you rarely see his shortcomings. To you, he's the same handsome, charming prince as the day you first met. And because of your sweet nature and abundance of affection and compassion—he treasures you as much. This is a form of compatibility, but to ensure that your relationship will continue on its golden path:

ADVICE

- Be sure to speak up when you're not happy with something.
- Take risks. Sometimes life requires a small "leap of faith." You'll feel good that you took some risks, even if they don't always work out as well as you hope. At least you can say you tried!
- Set personal goals. Decide what YOU would like to accomplish, set a schedule, and reward yourself in order to get you there.

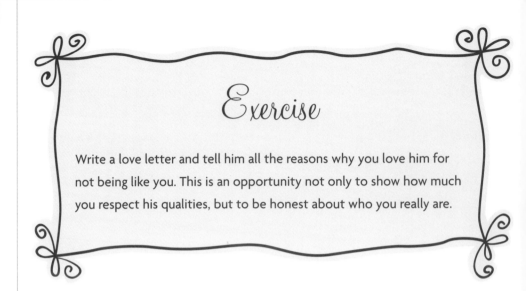

Exercise

Write a love letter and tell him all the reasons why you love him for not being like you. This is an opportunity not only to show how much you respect his qualities, but to be honest about who you really are.

"I love her too, but our neuroses
just don't match."

—ARTHUR MILLER

Where Do You See the Relationship in a Year?

Has the heat gone out of your romance? Are you fighting a lot? Have you found yourself sitting on the fence, wondering why the heck you're still in the relationship? Do you try breaking up only to find yourselves back in each other's arms? In other words, does your relationship really have a future, and is it worth all this angst? Take this test to find out whether your relationship has long-term potential or if you would be better off calling it quits.

1 **You can tell he's had another bad day at work. You:**

a. Let him vent.

b. Help him unwind by watching his favorite movie with him.

c. Walk out of the room.

2 **You tell him you love him:**

a. All the time.

b. Whenever the spirit moves you or you feel he needs a boost.

c. Well, actually you can't remember the last time.

3 **While walking in the park, you're more likely to be:**

a. Strolling side by side, deep in conversation.

b. Walking hand in hand in comfortable silence.

c. Checking out people of the opposite sex.

4 **When his birthday rolls around, will you:**

a. Ask him what his heart desires.

b. Surprise him.

c. Hope he doesn't expect anything.

5 After a disagreement, who usually apologizes first?

a. He does

b. You do

c. No one

6 Lately, he's been getting a little self-conscious about his physique. You:

a. Lift his spirits by telling him he looks better than ever to you.

b. Assure him you love him the way he is but encourage him to workout—if he's not happy with himself.

c. Tell him you've been noticing his flab, too.

7 When turning in for the night, you usually:

a. Snuggle for a bit.

b. Kiss each other and roll over to your respective sides.

c. Sleep on the couch.

8 How often do you and your mate get together with mutual friends?

a. Often

b. Once in a while

c. Rarely, if ever

9 When it comes to making household decisions, you:

a. Basically agree with each other.

b. Often have to compromise.

c. Decide on your own.

10 Which weekend getaway would you prefer?

a. Anywhere you can be together

b. Anywhere you can enjoy time apart and together

c. Anywhere you can be alone

Analysis

MOSTLY A'S
YOU HAVE A BRIGHT FUTURE—TOGETHER.

You truly adore each other and both lavish equal amounts of attention on each other every chance you get. Whether he's sharing his hard day or his dreams for the future, you get that it's important—and see yourself in his picture. Your relationship thrives in this loving bond that's been created through intimate conversations and passionate connections. Since you both cherish your moments together, it's clear that if you continue with the same mutual respect and compassion, your life together will be a long one. To help plan for the future:

ADVICE

- Work up a budget. Even in the best relationships money can be a sticky issue.
- Spend more time apart. It may sound contradictory, but couples that are so close can lose themselves. It's important to maintain your individual interests.
- Make a commitment to a cause outside yourselves. Since you have a future together, invest it in a worthy cause and volunteer with a charitable or political group. Studies show this kind of involvement will enhance your connection.

MOSTLY B'S
YOU UNDERSTAND EACH OTHER.

Whether you're watching TV, making a meal, or running errands together, you're both aware that you're in this together and are charmed by each other's company. Skilled at reading each other's emotions, you know when you need comforting and when it's best to be left alone. Most of the time it's clear that you're willing to make whatever compromises needed for this relationship to work, and he seems willing to do the same. Time will tell whether you're going to last for a lifetime, but for now, all indications are that it's certainly worth the effort. To make more of a commitment:

ADVICE

- Get a pet. Caring for an animal jointly will help you see how responsible he is and vice versa.
- Take a long trip together. Much is revealed during vacations, especially if they're rugged. You'll find out how you both weather the inevitable obstacles.
- Share a savings account. Agree to each put a small amount of money monthly into a joint account—and then when your goal is reached decide how you want to spend it. This is an excellent exercise to help reveal whether you see your financial future with the same vision.

MOSTLY C'S
YOU MAY HAVE TO RECONSIDER.

You believe in your hopes and dreams—and believe that willpower and perseverance will get you where you want to go. This grip on your destiny gives you a real sense of power and in fact, research shows that people who feel in control of their lives are psychologically happier. Unfortunately, there are clear warning signs that try as you might to keep your relationship going, it might not have much of a healthy future. You've got to reevaluate. Take off your rose-colored glasses and decide whether this relationship deserves any more of your precious time and energy. You may want it to go forward—but does he?

ADVICE

- Imagine your life without him. Consider the ways it might change for the better.
- Release the dream by writing it down and then letting the paper float away in the wind—or burn it.
- Surrender to whatever happens. Open your palms and feel the release from grasping.

Exercise

Marilyn Graman, author of *There is no Prince and Other Truths Your Mother Never Told You*, suggests asking these questions if you want to find out whether your relationship has a future:

- Is your honey willing to plan something two months down the road? If not, he may not be thinking beyond your next date.
- Does he ever talk about getting married or being in a long-term relationship? If he doesn't discuss it, he's probably not ready to think about the future.
- Also, don't ignore the signs just because you want to stay in a relationship. Be willing to ask if he thinks your relationship might end up going anywhere. But be prepared to consider moving on if he doesn't.
- And the final way to tell if you relationship has a future is to face the facts. Pay attention if he suddenly decides it's not a good time to meet your family, or he cancels your planned vacation to Bermuda. He may be rethinking your relationship, and you need to deal with it.

Counsel

HOW TO KEEP YOUR RELATIONSHIP
IN THE FORWARD-MOVING ZONE.

- Focus on solving problems instead of winning arguments.
- Listen with an open mind to make sure you understand what he means instead of launching into an unnecessary argument.
- Explain yourself if you feel you have been misunderstood.
- Respect each other's opinion, even if you can't find an immediate solution to the problem.
- Spend time discussing problems and issues you each think are important.
- Be quick to forgive *and* quick to forget.
- Be sincere. Your words may say one thing, but your body language may convey something completely different.
- Don't talk in code. Say what you mean, and say it respectfully.
- Don't go to sleep before resolving a conflict.

"Couples break up because of decreased levels
of satisfaction in the relationship—not
because they stop loving each other."

—SUSAN SPRECHER, PSYCHOLOGIST

View the Positive Side of Your Relationship—In the Movies!

Depending upon where you point your lens, a relationship can appear to be a full-fledged romance or a fatal attraction. After all, our perceptions are what guide us. In fact, research shows that our classic romantic movie-match can actually identify the best parts of our own relationship. Take this quiz developed with Carolyn Kaufman, Psy.D., a clinical and media psychologist, and discover which film reveals the upside of your guy.

1 **The last time you were working on a big clean-up project together, you:**
a. Put the task on your calendar and got to it on the date set.
b. Did it bit by bit until the job was finished.
c. Tackled it on a whim.

2 **If he were trying out a new route home and you ended up lost, would it likely mean:**
a. He would return to the tried and true route the next time.
b. He'd learn from his mistake and try again.
c. He'd laugh about it and ask your advice.

3 **If you were going to take a class together, would you choose:**
a. A seminar on something practical.
b. An inspirational workshop on making dreams come true.
c. A creative hands-on class where you could collaborate.

4 **If you were worried you weren't going to remember an important appointment, could you rely on him to:**
a. Remind you ahead of time.
b. Ask about it after the fact.
c. Forget about it, too.

5 What would you guys wear for a night out on the town?

a. Something understated and tailored

b. Put on the Ritz in an elegant way

c. Fun, attention-getting outfits

6 His favorite real-life stories are about:

a. Making noble choices that help others.

b. Persevering in spite of difficulties.

c. Finding happiness in any situation.

7 When the phone rings, who reaches for it first?

a. He does

b. You do

c. Usually both, simultaneously

8 You're especially proud of his:

a. Courage and dedication to his dreams.

b. Loyalty to loved ones.

c. Playfulness and sense of adventure.

9 The biggest life lesson your relationship can help you remember is:

a. Doing what is right can be more rewarding than doing what you want.

b. You should never let go of your dreams.

c. Laughter can be more important than romance.

10 You would prefer to spend time with him:

a. Working on a worthy cause.

b. Designing a creative project.

c. Frolicking on the beach.

Analysis

MOSTLY A'S

IF YOUR RELATIONSHIP WAS A MOVIE IT WOULD BE *CASABLANCA.*

As a genuinely noble woman like Ilsa Lund, the heroine of *Casablanca*, your high ideals and commitment to always do the right thing keeps you centered and taking the high road. Your man meets you there in the same way that Rick Blaine sets aside his wild side to reach his higher self. "Practical yet warm-hearted and down-to-earth, his priority is putting the well-being of those he loves first—and of course that means you!" says Kaufman. And he keeps his eye on the prize—willing to make sacrifices to reach important long-term goals.

ADVICE

- Help him to put himself first more often. Run a bath or offer a massage. Studies confirm we have more to give to others when we're taking care of our own needs first.

MOSTLY B'S

IF YOUR RELATIONSHIP WAS A MOVIE IT WOULD BE *GONE WITH THE WIND.*

Just like the strong-willed and romantic Scarlet O'Hara, who does what she must to keep her home and family in tact, your Rhett believes in hopes and dreams and knows that willpower and perseverance gets him where he needs to go. Having a grip on destiny gives your man a real sense of power. He is a happy guy when he believes he is in control of his life. Feeling so confident can lead your man to multitask.

ADVICE

- To help him stay in balance, suggest he keep a list of priorities and limit his daily to-do list to four tasks. That way he'll have more time to spend with you.

MOSTLY C'S
IF YOUR RELATIONSHIP WAS A MOVIE IT WOULD BE
THE SOUND OF MUSIC.

It doesn't take long for Captain Von Trapp and his seven unruly children to fall in love with Maria, their playful and musical new governess. Just like Maria, you're loveable with a lively spirit, a good sense of humor, and the ability to find something positive in any situation. It's the same for your man. Your common ground is your shared carefree, fun-loving outlook on life. The sound of laughter is one of your favorite things—and that's why you appreciate his light-hearted approach to problems. Another bonus: laughter and optimism increase life expectancy.

ADVICE

· Everyone experiences a case of the blues once in a while, so if he has a bad day here and there, don't twist yourself into a knot. It's healthy to experience a wide range of emotions. And that goes for you, too.

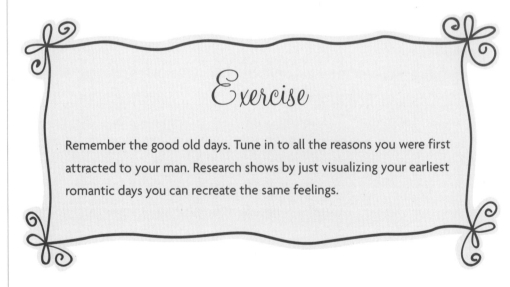

Exercise

Remember the good old days. Tune in to all the reasons you were first attracted to your man. Research shows by just visualizing your earliest romantic days you can recreate the same feelings.

"Love is not enough. It must be the foundation, the cornerstone—but not the complete structure. It is much too pliable, too yielding."

—BETTE DAVIS

Who Comes First?

Sure, we want to be loved. "But if you end up sacrificing your own happiness for everyone else's it can ultimately take a toll on your self-esteem and sense of well-being," says psychologist Diana Kirschner, PhD, author of *Opening Love's Door: The Seven Lessons.* Take this test to see if it's in your nature to try too hard to please others—especially your partner—and then get tips on how to boost your personal resolve so you can put yourself first.

1 **If you were at a dinner party and found yourself disagreeing with your host's views, you would probably:**
a. Still stress your point of view.
b. Keep the conversation pleasant, even if it means conceding.
c. Politely smile and nod.

2 **If the person ahead of you on the supermarket express aisle had more than the items allotted, would you:**
a. Suggest she move to a regular line.
b. Point it out, but let her proceed.
c. Either go to another line or say nothing.

3 **If your boyfriend asked whether you liked the shirt he was wearing . . . and really, you didn't, would you probably:**
a. Tell him the honest truth so he wouldn't wear it again.
b. Sugarcoat your opinion by stressing the positive.
c. Tell a white lie and say, "You look great!"

4 **When you're out with buddies for lunch, you usually offer to:**
a. Pay your portion.
b. Split the bill evenly.
c. Either pick up the entire tab or pay the full tip in addition to your portion.

5 If your partner says something that's hurtful, are you most likely to:

a. Tell him he hurt your feelings.

b. Offer a cold shoulder until your feelings heal.

c. Simply hope it doesn't happen again.

6 Who are you most likely to impulse buy a gift for?

a. Yourself

b. Sometimes yourself, but more often your partner

c. Always him

7 When talking to people in positions of authority, you feel nervous:

a. Almost never.

b. Sometimes.

c. Often.

8 If during a staff meeting, a colleague presents one of your ideas as his or her own, would you most likely:

a. Express your displeasure immediately—and take the credit you deserve.

b. Say nothing in front of the group, but point out your resentment privately.

c. Tell her you're flattered she likes *your* idea.

9 On an average day, you apologize to your guy:

a. Once or twice, if at all.

b. About five times.

c. Between six and a dozen or more times.

10 When it comes to making love, would you describe yourself as:

a. The initiator.

b. The mentor.

c. The follower.

11 If you were served cold soup or coffee at a restaurant, you would be most likely to:

a. Send it back.

b. Leave it untouched.

c. Drink it anyway.

12 Pride is . . .

a. An important quality to possess.

b. Something you try not to cultivate.

c. A personality flaw.

13 When an argument with your lover is over, how often do you replay the situation in your head, thinking of all the things you could have said?

a. Almost never

b. Sometimes

c. Often

Analysis

MOSTLY A'S
YOU STICK TO YOUR GUNS.

Supremely self-confident, you're able to express your honest feelings and assert your beliefs even if someone disagrees. "Research confirms people aren't born with this kind of inner strength—it's *learned*," says Kirschner. "You were raised in a nurturing home with respect for your abilities and plenty of opportunities to take charge." Your gung-ho independence is admirable, but in relationships compromise is not only appropriate—it's imperative. To nurture a more flexible strength:

ADVICE

- Use reflective listening. Research shows if you listen carefully not only to what is being said, but also to what is meant—without thinking of your response—you'll be twice as likely to come to a compromise.
- Take a yoga, stretch, or dance class. Studies of the mind-body connection point to a correlation between physical and mental flexibility.
- Ask yourself: "What's the worst thing that can happen if I don't get my way?" Fiercely independent types often feel they have to control their partners because they're sure what's right. Give yourself the opportunity to explore other possibilities and consider you might not always be right.

MOSTLY B'S
YOU KNOW HOW TO JUGGLE EVERYONE'S NEEDS.

As a truly compassionate soul, you can slip easily into another's shoes. That's why your goal is to create a "win-win" outcome for your loved ones. "Folks in this category concentrate so intensely on fairness—weighing pros and cons of every issue," says Kirschner, "they often end up skewing a decision just so their mate's needs are met—even if it's not the best or right way to go." When you need to take a strong position:

ADVICE

- Go with your gut reaction. Kirschner says, "Women in this category are often run by their intellect." When you have an inspiration or intuitive spark—go for it!
- Laugh more. Release yourself from the pressure of being absolutely fair by keeping a sense of humor about it. Remind yourself: "I'm not Judge Judy!"
- Visualize saying no in front of a mirror . . . and stand tall! Research shows just by practicing assertiveness and resolve, you'll gain the confidence to take a stand without feelings of guilt or remorse.

MOSTLY C'S
YOU ALWAYS PUT HIM FIRST
(AND OFTEN FORGET YOURSELF!).

Deep down you want nothing more than to be loved and cherished. "Our studies show people who have this strong drive for approval and love," says Kirschner, "won very little acceptance as children—and now want to make up for lost time." But when you give up on your own desires or say yes when you want to say no there's a good chance resentment, anger, or depression will build up. Remember the old adage, "To thine own self be true." It's the only way to be truly happy. To practice putting yourself first:

ADVICE

- Take tiny steps; say no to small requests first. For example, say: "I can't get you water now. I'll get it in a few minutes, or you can get it yourself."
- Practice loving and giving to yourself. When you have the urge to buy a gift for your boyfriend—get one for yourself instead! Or be sure to be make time for relaxation and pampering. You deserve it.
- Keep a photo of yourself as a baby in view. Studies show this simple technique will help you focus on protecting and loving your innocent, beautiful self.

Exercise

- Acknowledge your strengths. Do things that bring your strengths out into the open. If you're a good baker, why not make dessert the crowning achievement of a candlelit dinner?
- Learn to accept compliments. It's hard to accept a compliment. But remember: if someone is thinking well of you—then you should, too.
- Get in shape. Eat healthy, exercise, and get plenty of rest. When you take care of yourself your physical and emotional health will improve. You'll be able to think more clearly and feel better about yourself and your decisions.

FACTOID

Women are 80 percent more likely to point out possible mistakes by saying, "You're right, but maybe it could be . . ." Whereas a man's response is more likely to be "I'm sorry, but you're wrong," or even more direct just plain . . . "You're wrong."

"You yourself, as much as anybody in the entire universe, deserve your love and affection."

—BUDDHA

Are Your Problems Too Big to Ignore?

Of course, it's only human to get irritated. According to a Hofstra University study, most of us report feeling some degree of pique at least a few times a week—and when it's focused and directed it can be positive. "Healthy rancor can mobilize you to take action, set limits to the demands others make, think about why something matters so much, or defend yourself if attacked," says Tony Hope, MD, a psychiatrist, professor of medical ethics, and author of *Managing Your Mind: The Mental Fitness Guide.* But he also cautions, "It can blind you to other ways of seeing things, understanding what's really important, sharing responsibility, and finding peaceful options to dealing with real or imagined difficulties." Plus, it can blur the line between small, inconsequential annoyances, and big problems that shouldn't be ignored. This test will help you discover which kinds of difficulties your relationship is really maneuvering around—and offer advice on what you can do about it.

1 **When you're having difficulty solving a problem—whether it's paying your taxes or finding your keys, he:**

a. Offers his help.

b. Ignores your sighs.

c. Accused you of being a scatterbrain—or worse.

2 **When shopping together for a big-ticket, or even a small item, the decisions are:**

a. Left up to you.

b. An exercise in compromise.

c. Ultimately, *his* choice,

3 **If you're feeling dissed, you:**

a. Say so right away.

b. Eventually share your feelings.

c. Keep it to yourself.

4 **How often would you say the two of you argue?**

a. Rarely

b. Once or twice a week

c. Constantly—at least a few times each day

5 **How does he express his anger?**

a. By talking it over

b. By getting all sullen

c. By ranting and raving—sometimes throwing things or threatening you

6 **Do you trust him to stay true blue?**

a. Absolutely

b. As much as you can trust any man

c. Not at all. His history proves he's a player.

7 **How often do you have sex?**

a. At least three or four times a week

b. Once or twice a week

c. Pretty sporadically

8 **And when you do make love, how sensitive would you say he is to your satisfaction?**

a. Very, very, *very!!!*

b. A fair amount

c. Not nearly enough

9 **How often do you contact each other during the day when you're apart?**

a. A few times

b. At least once

c. Rarely

10. **If you had a burning secret, would you share it with him?**

a. Of course

b. Probably

c. I doubt it

11. **If he came into an inheritance, he would probably:**

a. Ask you how you think it should be managed.

b. Buy you a lovely present and save a chunk.

c. Blow it on stuff for him.

12. **When it comes to tidiness, his habits:**

a. Fit in perfectly with your own.

b. Conflict a little with yours.

c. He's Oscar to your Felix or vice versa.

Analysis

MOSTLY A'S

THERE ARE NO INSURMOUNTABLE ISSUES.

Nothing is perfect in life and, of course, you'll occasionally argue over the big stuff—and the small stuff, too. But that's okay because the fundamental foundation of your relationship is solid. Your differences aren't gaping divides, and you come together more often than you drift apart. You share values and see the world the same way—and there's an undercurrent of mutual respect, which gives the fabric of your relationship flexibility and strength. When there's a problem, each of you knows how to discuss it like adults—keeping an open mind and holding back judgment. Your views on money run along similar lines. And when it comes to sex, he's there to please, as are you. This give and take is exactly what a healthy relationship possesses. No matter what issues arise, they'll easily be overcome. Here's the only real sticky point:

sometimes you just don't feel like sharing *all* your problems with him. That's okay. But don't keep it to yourself. Instead:

ADVICE

- Open up to a true friend. Talk it over with someone who has your best interests in mind. Be sure your confidant is both supportive *and* honest.

WHY THIS WORKS:

Women tend to ruminate, and then they end up either rationalizing their anger or blaming themselves for the outburst. "By sharing your story with a friend who really knows who you are, she can enable you to gain perspective, see the situation from a different angle, and help you to accept your emotions," says Eve A. Wood, MD, author of *10 Steps to Take Charge of Your Emotional Life*. "Also, by giving voice to your story, the emotional charge behind it gets diluted." Even better, a good friend can suggest ways you might handle the conflict differently.

MOSTLY B'S
YOU RELATIONSHIP MAY BE A LITTLE TOO BLASÉ.

Where's the fire? Each of you is playing the dance of avoidance rather than dealing with problems that may or may not be important. Sometimes it's risky to take a stand, or dig around in the muck, or search for the truth, but in order for a relationship to stay vibrant and alive, you need to take chances—put your issues out there. A middle-of-the-road attitude keeps you both at a sort of way station. There is such a thing as too much compromise and that's what's going on here. It may be an indication that you're not willing to move onto the next level of commitment. Here's what you can do:

ADVICE

- Dare to admit how you're really feeling. Simply say the words "I'm feeling angry."

WHY THIS WORKS:

Anger needs to be named and acknowledged before you can move through it. "If it isn't identified, you're more likely to stuff the feeling, giving it the chance to evolve into another emotion such as frustration, stress, or sadness. Or you might numb the feeling with a self-defeating action like overeating," cautions Martha Straus, PhD, author of *Adolescent Girls in Crisis: Intervention and Hope.* "Naming it is the first step to releasing (not unleashing) your rancor."

MOSTLY C'S
THE RELATIONSHIP STILL HAS LOTS OF PASSION BUT . . .

It's been channeled into anger and resentment. The result is too much fighting and not enough fun. The bigger underlying problem is stress. This issue could be handled if you both came together like a team. But that's not the dynamic. Instead of standing up for what you believe in, you've let him bully you. Your reaction is to keep your resentment to yourself—and it builds up. The likelihood that eventually one of you is going to look for a more intimate relationship with less stress is pretty high. But like most problems, it can be solved.

ADVICE

- Let go of resentment. This doesn't mean believing what the other person did was right or justified; it means you stop wasting your energy staying mad and understand all the disadvantages of doing so. If an apology is offered, accept it and avoid dwelling on the wrong that was done.

WHY THIS WORKS:

The urge to let bygones be bygones is shared by most all of us, but few of us actually know how to forgive. "As long as we hold on to a grudge, we can never forgive others, and our lack of forgiveness hurts no one but ourselves," explains Thubten Chodron, Buddhist teacher and spiritual advisor. But absolution isn't easy; it takes time and intention. It also means changing the way we think. The reward, however, is undeniable. "As soon as you understand your reaction is your own responsibility," says Thubten Chodren, "you're no longer handing your power over to anyone else—you're the one in charge."

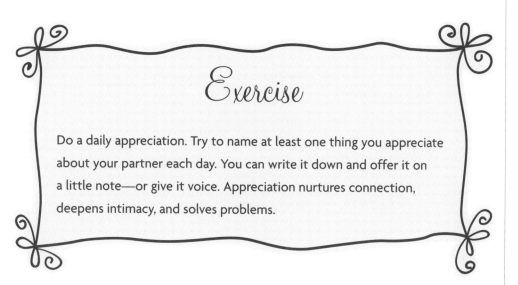

Exercise

Do a daily appreciation. Try to name at least one thing you appreciate about your partner each day. You can write it down and offer it on a little note—or give it voice. Appreciation nurtures connection, deepens intimacy, and solves problems.

"Most people spend more time and energy going around problems than in trying to solve them."

—HENRY FORD

What's the Main Problem?

Not too surprisingly, a poll by MarriageAdvice.com reveals couples mostly fight about sex and money. But scratch the surface and most relationship problems go deeper to what I call the *Huge Five:*

1) Dealing with unresolved issues from the past
2) Believing you're misunderstood
3) Taking the relationship for granted
4) Cheating, jealousy, and other trust issues
5) Allowing arguments to escalate to dangerous ground

If any of these issues sound *too* familiar, don't despair. The first step in fixing problems is identifying them. Once that's accomplished, you can put solutions into practice.

PART ONE

1. Basically, you're attracted to a certain kind of guy. He's . . .

a. Just like the very first love of your life—in every way.

b. The quiet type.

c. An artist.

d. A player.

e. A risk-taker.

2. You've been spending time with a guy you like, and he tells you that he does not want a committed relationship. Do you think:

a. He may think that now, but he won't be able to resist me for long.

b. Still waters run deep. He's feeling it but he needs a little coaxing.

c. It doesn't matter. I can devote myself to him on his terms.

d. Bring on the competition!

e. I'll offer unforgettable nights of lovemaking so he won't stray.

3 As a teenager, what kind of TV shows did you prefer to watch?

a. Family dramas

b. Sappy romance shows

c. Celebrity gossip

d. Hot soap operas

e. Adventure shows

4 ... and now, when you read the Sunday newspaper, do you turn first to the:

a. Obituaries

b. Wedding announcements

c. Arts and culture section

d. Lifestyle pages

e. Current news

5 On the average, how long do you usually date someone?

a. More than five years

b. More than two years

c. More than a year

d. More than six months

c. Two months at most

6 You start a new job and you immediately fall for a guy in the office—who is already in a relationship. What do you do?

a. Flirt

b. Just fantasize

c. Wait for him to make the first move

d. Let it go

e. Go for it—and watch the cards fall where they may.

7 If you're feeling a little down, you'll put on something:

a. Cotton and get comfy.

b. Cashmere to feel luxurious.

c. Silk and satin because feeling sensuous will perk you up.

d. Lace and velvet for a sexy pick-me-up.

e. Anything denim to knock around the house in.

8 How do you feel about love?

a. It's the greatest thing a person can have.

b. It's all about communication.

c. It needs to be cultivated if you want it to last.

d. If you keep your heart open, it's always available.

e. You've got to fight for it.

Analysis

MOSTLY A'S

YOUR BIG PROBLEM IS DEALING WITH UNRESOLVED ISSUES FROM THE PAST.

Many people go from relationship to relationship without truly healing their hearts. They never discover what went wrong in their previous relationship and what they could have done differently. Of course, they keep repeating the same mistakes over and over again—yet expecting a different outcome. Ring a bell?

ADVICE

· Take the time to heal your broken heart and your attachment to being a victim—or whatever holds you to a previous relationship.

· Take responsibility for what happened.

· Forgive yourself and your previous partner.

· Make a to-do list of what you want to change in your life.

MOSTLY B'S
YOUR BIGGEST PROBLEM IS THAT YOU
FEEL AS IF YOU'RE MISUNDERSTOOD.

It's to be expected that being in an intimate relationship will inevitably bring up fears and challenges. These might include fears of not being good enough, attractive enough, or feeling that your partner doesn't know the real *you*. If your fears are not expressed, looked at, and healed, they will interfere with the health of your relationship.

ADVICE

- Notice when fears surface, and instead of looking outward and blaming your partner, consider whether it's *your* issue.
- Ask yourself if you're really being neglected or are you just making stories up in your head.
- If you feel strongly that you're not being understood, set aside a specific time to talk to your lover about your concerns. Practice in front of a mirror first so that you feel comfortable expressing your true feelings.
- If talking about it is too tough, write a letter explaining your concerns. Avoid blaming him. After all, if you're feeling misunderstood it may be because you haven't been honest about who you are and what you expect and need from the relationship.

MOSTLY C'S
YOUR BIGGEST PROBLEM IS THAT YOU
TAKE THE RELATIONSHIP FOR GRANTED.

We're working longer hours (or freaked out about losing our jobs), multitasking to the max, and generally spending less time with our partners than ever before. When we're tired, communication is cut down to the bare essentials with conversations like "What time will you be back?" as you cross paths in the kitchen. In the past, couples would stay up half the night fighting and probably solve the argument; today they are too aware of that early meeting to want to waste precious sleep time. Instead we complain that our partner never listens.

ADVICE

- Set aside "sacred time" that belongs to just the two of you. For example, make Thursday night your date night. Even if you can't go out, spend the time talking, listening to music, or making love. FYI: Many couples in therapy find they benefit most from the concentrated, quality time they spend together, rather than the counseling.
- Don't make assumptions, but check out your hunches. If you think you know what's going on in your partner's mind and heart, there's a good chance you're at least slightly off base. Ask questions and really listen.
- Write a love letter. Tell him all the reason you love him.
- Rekindle your initial feelings of attraction by remembering what it was like the day you knew he was the one for you.

MOSTLY D'S
YOUR BIGGEST PROBLEM IS ALL ABOUT TRUST.

Occasional jealousy is natural and can help keep a relationship lively, but if it becomes intense and irrational it can put a dangerous strain on the relationship. Your partner ends up feeling as though he's constantly walking on eggshells to avoid a jealous reaction. The jealous partner, often aware of their problem, swings between self-blame and justification. If your partner is in fact cheating you should seriously consider ending the relationship. But if it's really *your* trust issue, you need to work on it.

ADVICE

- Give yourself a reality check—take a good look at those things that trigger your jealousy and ask yourself how realistic the threat is. What evidence do you have that your relationship is in danger? And is your behavior actually making the situation worse?

- Use positive self-talk—when you start feeling the twinges of jealousy, remind yourself that your partner loves you, is committed to you, and respects you. Tell yourself you're a loveable person and that nothing's going on.
- Seek reassurance—one of the best ways to beat jealousy is to ask your partner for reassurance. Make sure you don't nag or bully, but rather share your insecurities and ask him to help you overcome the problem.

MOSTLY E'S
YOUR BIGGEST PROBLEM IS ALLOWING ARGUMENTS TO ESCALATE.

One of the most common mistakes people in a relationship make is to create absolute right or wrong scenarios. As soon as critical words are said, defenses and walls go up and suddenly that person (who you love and who loves you) becomes an "enemy." When arguments start getting out of hand, become accusatory, and escalate to blaming and name-calling, serious damage is done. Words can heal, but they can also be brutally destructive.

ADVICE
- Before you jump into blaming and judging your partner, stop and take a moment to breathe. Ask yourself if making your partner wrong will drive you further apart or move you closer toward healing.
- Try to understand the dynamics of what's going on between the two of you. Hear the full story before deciding he's wrong.
- Don't name-call. Once you've said something it's tough to take it back.
- If an apology is offered, work toward forgiveness rather than instantly dismissing it. If you've made a mistake, offer an apology.

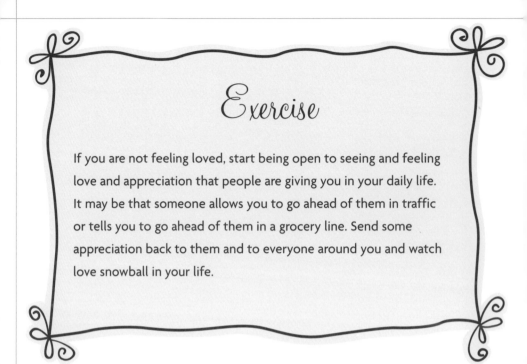

Exercise

If you are not feeling loved, start being open to seeing and feeling love and appreciation that people are giving you in your daily life. It may be that someone allows you to go ahead of them in traffic or tells you to go ahead of them in a grocery line. Send some appreciation back to them and to everyone around you and watch love snowball in your life.

"Hearts will never be practical until they are made unbreakable."

—THE WIZARD OF OZ

Who Starts Fights?

In most relationships someone takes the lead, and the other follows. But when a couple is in sync they come to a natural give-and-take; they're able to switch roles depending on the circumstances. It's not so easy when it comes to fighting. All couples argue, but different personality types approach conflict in different ways. By knowing who takes the lead, you can learn to deal with conflict in a positive way and develop a stronger relationship with your partner.

1 **When you're arguing you tend to:**
a. Throw out a zinger and then retreat.
b. Continue with a steady insistence.
c. Sulk.

2 **Imagine you've done something that really annoys your guy. He will most likely:**
a. Not say anything until days later.
b. Give you the cold shoulder.
c. Let you know.

3 **If he were late for dinner, would you:**
a. Stomp out of the kitchen. Let him fend for himself!
b. Let your displeasure be known—through every course.
c. Ask what happened.

4 **When you're arguing, who holds the strongest eye contact?**
a. I do.
b. He does.
c. We both do!

5 Who has the louder voice?

a. I do.

b. He does.

c. We're pretty well matched.

6 If you broke a promise, your partner would most likely:

a. Bring it up again and again.

b. Be pissed in the moment—but then let it go.

c. Be angry and disappointed but hear out your reasoning.

7 Who usually initiates the make-up after an argument?

a. He does.

b. I do.

c. It depends on who was wrong.

8 Who is more sarcastic?

a. I am.

b. He is.

c. Neither of us. It's not our style.

9 What do you focus on most when you're fighting?

a. Getting your point across

b. Staying calm

c. Resolving the disagreement quickly and fairly

10 As a couple, which of these statements is most true?

a. Fighting is the biggest way we communicate.

b. Fighting is unpleasant for me. I think my partner is more into it.

c. Fighting is an inevitable part of any relationship—but I'd prefer it if we didn't do it.

11 When you were growing up, who had a worse temper?

a. Mom

b. Dad

c. Neither had a bad temper

12 Does your partner belittle your opinions?

a. Rarely

b. Often

c. Almost never

13 If your partner did something really stupid in front of another couple, you would:

a. Call him on it right then and there. It's just too bad if he's embarrassed.

b. Shoot him a dirty look.

c. Bring it up as soon as you're alone with him.

Analysis

MOSTLY A'S
YOU'RE THE INSTIGATOR.

For some people, the inability to get along with others is a sign of a deeper emotional or personality issue. However, since you're generally an easy-going person who gets along with people, and usually has a good relationship with the man you're with, your style of losing your temper, instigating arguments, and resenting yourself for making reasonable compromises are some of the ways you have learned to cope with the stress of emotional closeness. You probably acquired this pattern while growing up, observing other people (possibly your parents and older siblings) mishandle stress and disagreements.

The good news is that you can change. The first step is recognizing your issue. The next one is changing the way you approach disagreements.

ADVICE

- Stay on point. Friendly fighting sticks with the issue. Neither party resorts to name-calling or character assassination. It's enough to deal with the problem without adding the new setback of hurting each other's feelings.
- Keep your voice down. The louder someone yells, the less likely they are to be heard. Even if your partner yells, there's no need to yell back. Taking the volume down makes it possible for people to start focusing on the issues instead of reacting to the noise.
- Soften your defenses. Defending yourself, whether by vehemently protesting your innocence and rightness or by turning the tables and attacking, escalates the fight. Instead of upping the ante, ask for more information, details, and examples. There is usually some basis for the other person's complaint. When you meet a complaint with curiosity, you make room for understanding.

MOSTLY B'S

HE'S THE INSTIGATOR.

Ongoing anger in a relationship is shown in two main ways. 1) Your partner seems to be permanently annoyed and simmers quietly but constantly, and 2) Your partner erupts and explodes with anger at the slightest thing. Violence or threats of violence are never all right in a relationship. If arguments are always aggressive, or you avoid conflict because you're scared of things getting out of control, then you should seek help at once. However your partner expresses their anger, the following tips will help you to minimize its destructive effect on you and your relationship.

ADVICE

- Acknowledge your partner's feelings. Openly saying, "I can see you're angry," and if appropriate, "I understand what you're angry about," will prevent your partner from believing they have to prove how they feel.
- Show you're listening. People often continue to be angry because they

don't think they're being listened to or taken seriously. Prevent this by giving eye contact, nodding and repeating significant words, and summarizing what's been said.

- Share your feelings and fears. If you're feeling angry, too, then say so. If you're feeling nervous or upset by their anger, then share that also.

MOSTLY C'S
YOU'RE IN THIS TOGETHER.

No two people in the world will ever agree about everything at all times. (It would be boring if they did.) So couples do need to know how to negotiate differences and make room for constructive criticism. They also need a way to assert opinions, disagree, and have a healthy way to express intense feelings. A good relationship requires knowing the skills necessary for "friendly fighting"—dealing with conflict respectfully and working together to find a workable solution. Friendly fighting means working out differences that matter. It means engaging passionately about things we feel strongly about, without resorting to hurting each other. It helps us let off steam without getting burned. Friendly fighting lets us "fight" and still stay friends. Here's how to do it:

ADVICE

- Embrace conflict. There is no need to fear it. Conflict is normal, even healthy. Differences between you mean that there are things you can learn from each other.
- Find points of agreement. Almost always there are parts of a conflict that can be points of agreement. Finding common ground, even if it's agreeing that there is a problem, is an important start to finding a common solution.
- Make concessions. Small concessions can turn the situation around. If you give a little, it makes room for the other person to make concessions, too. Small concessions lead to larger compromises. Compromise doesn't

have to mean that you're meeting each other exactly 50–50. Sometimes it's a 60–40 or even an 80–20 agreement. This isn't about scorekeeping. It's about finding a solution that is workable for both of you.

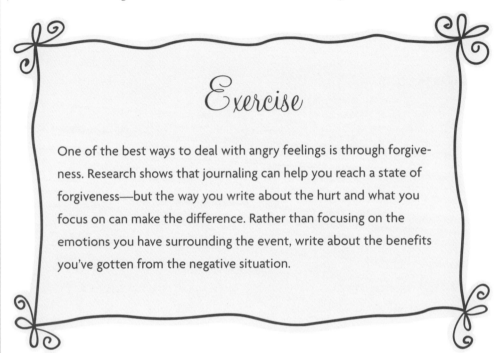

Exercise

One of the best ways to deal with angry feelings is through forgiveness. Research shows that journaling can help you reach a state of forgiveness—but the way you write about the hurt and what you focus on can make the difference. Rather than focusing on the emotions you have surrounding the event, write about the benefits you've gotten from the negative situation.

"Be calm in arguing for fierceness makes error a fault, and truth discourtesy."

—GEORGE HERBERT

Where do you stand on the G.S.—Grudge Scale?

On some level it has to feel good to hold a grudge. If it didn't, why would so many couples cling to theirs? But here's a reality check: although we may get fleeting satisfaction from staying pissed off, acting passive-aggressively, or holding fast and furiously to a grudge, it has long-lasting toxic effects on our relationship. If you are unable to let go of a grudge, you can spend years feeling emotionally bitter and resentful. You can even get physically sick! Studies show anger increases heart rate, elevates blood pressure, and makes you depressed. To set a grudge free, you first have to see it—and then figure out the strategy that will work best for you and your relationship. Dr. Katherine Piderman, the staff chaplain at the famed Mayo Clinic, says, "Letting go of a grudge doesn't mean you're condoning a hurtful action, or excusing bad behavior; it means you're moving on so that you can put emotional control back in your own hands." This will heal your heart. Take the first step with this quiz and find out where you land on the grudge scale.

1 **I share my deepest worries, thoughts, and emotions with my partner and believe he is attentive and understanding.**
a. Often   b. Sometimes   c. Rarely

2 **When my partner is talking to me about *his* problems, I'm open to what he is saying and won't form a judgment or interrupt him in order to share my viewpoint.**
a. Often   b. Sometimes   c. Rarely

3 **If I'm freaking out about something (raising my voice, making threats, getting hysterical), I realize it pretty quickly, offer an apology, and try to dampen my reaction.**
a. Often   b. Sometimes   c. Rarely

4 If my partner says something that hurts me, as soon as he's done speaking I let him know how I'm feeling and why.

a. Often   b. Sometimes   c. Rarely

5 I'd rather ask questions about how my partner is feeling than assume I know what's going on.

a. Often   b. Sometimes   c. Rarely

6 Also, I try to ask them in an open-ended way without any preconceptions.

a. Often   b. Sometimes   c. Rarely

7 If it was a matter of keeping the peace, I would opt to find a compromise rather than coerce my partner into conceding. Winning isn't my goal.

a. Often   b. Sometimes   c. Rarely

8 Besides my partner, I share my honest beliefs, thoughts, and fears with close friends.

a. Often   b. Sometimes   c. Rarely

9 If a trusted friend gave me advice about my relationship problems, I'd take his or her perspective seriously.

a. Often   b. Sometimes   c. Rarely

10 Rather than ruminate or feel resentful, if my partner isn't doing his share around the house or holding up his other responsibilities, I let him know.

a. Often   b. Sometimes   c. Rarely

11 Our relationship has plenty of carefree, loving moments.

a. Often   b. Sometimes   c. Rarely

12 I know the sore points that will get my partner going. If it isn't crucial to solving a problem, I try to avoid them.
a. Often   b. Sometimes   c. Rarely

13 I believe my partner can be trusted.
a. Often   b. Sometimes   c. Rarely

14 Whenever I'm authentically feeling gratitude toward my partner and our relationship, I express it—no holds barred.
a. Often   b. Sometimes   c. Rarely

15 Truthfully, I see a long and happy future together.
a. Often   b. Sometimes   c. Rarely

Analysis

MOSTLY A'S
YOU'RE PRACTICALLY GRUDGE-FREE!

You scored exceptionally low on the G.S. and have a natural, almost reflexive ability to forgive transgressions and move on. In fact, when faced with injustice, you're more likely to feel sorrow than anger. But be careful: You're so trusting and quick to look at the upside that you're sometimes blind to your partner's faults. What's the problem? Well, it could mean you're avoiding dealing with an issue that needs work. On the other hand, a nature as truly forgiving as yours saves you from stress created by frustration and resentment. If you place a little caution alongside your compassion, you're likely to live a joyful life together. Here are tips to keep you in balance.

ADVICE

- Don't forgive until you are really ready. You don't want to be sweeping your feelings under a rug of hidden resentment.
- Ask for an apology. Although it's not a good idea to focus on righting the wrong by getting an apology, it's certainly okay to ask for one.
- Talk to someone. If your partner has done you wrong, discuss it with a trusted friend and get his or her viewpoint. Sometimes your forgiving nature can be a little over the top.

MOSTLY B'S
YOU'RE REASONABLE.

Your score on the G.S. shows that you have a balanced approach to anger and tend to step back and look at the bigger picture rather than get bogged down in tiny slights. You rarely take offense at your partner's minor transgressions and, more often than not, let bygones be bygones. Resentment is just not a feeling you frequently experience. However, since you're not a saint, some things do get under your skin. You're a stickler for honesty and find it easier to forgive your partner when he comes clean than when he denies or tries to cover up his mistakes. But good riddance to the guy who dares to cheat on you! Otherwise, in most matters of the heart, your motto is "To err is human."

ADVICE

- Write down your thoughts. Think about what upsets you and how you feel about it. Writing can keep your perspective in focus.
- Consider possible motives. Often our partners say and do things in fits of anger (or another intense emotion) and later regret it. If the offense is forgivable—forgive and try to forget.
- Revisit the honesty thing. Sometimes our partners lie out of embarrassment or a lack of self-confidence. Try to investigate his motive before racing to a conclusion.

MOSTLY C'S
YOU'RE A GRUDGE-AHOLIC.

When you feel wronged, you're merciless. In fact, no matter how sincerely your partner offers an apology, you're apt to ignore his gesture. Sometimes (depending on the seriousness of the offense), you may take it a step further and resolve to get even. This is a lose-lose situation because grudge holding makes you miserable and sucks the energy out of your life. But don't get all down on yourself. There may be a reason for your hard heart; as a child you were probably given the same sour treatment. Now, as an adult, you cherish a grudge as if it were a valuable gem. Forgiveness is the balm that heals old wounds. Now is the time to open your heart and let the diamond shine. Here are some ways you can learn to let go of what has a nasty hold on you:

ADVICE

- Remind yourself that letting go of a grudge does not mean you stuff your feelings away. It means changing how you think about the situation. You can't change what happened, but you can change your attitude and interpretation of events.
- Don't focus on righting the wrong—or getting revenge. Although this is a common reaction of grudge-holders, it's a destructive pattern. Instead, practice releasing your anger through exercise, talk therapy, or deep breathing and meditation.
- Remind yourself that you're not perfect. How many times have you made a mistake?

Exercise

HAVE A HEARTY HA-HA-HA!

Try a one-minute laugh riot and get the same grudge and stress-busting benefits of a forty-five-minute workout at the gym. No kidding! According to a recent German study conducted by gelotologist (one who studies laughter) Gunther Sickl, MD, when we laugh out loud, oxygen and stress-relieving hormones surge through the body making us feel carefree; it's similar to the effect of a runner's "high."

"I've had a few arguments with people, but I never carry a grudge. You know why? While you're carrying a grudge, they're out dancing."

—BUDDY HACKETT

Is Your Relationship Worth Saving?

When a relationship gets rocky, it's tough to figure out whether salvaging it is worth the heartache, effort, or time. It often feels overwhelming. Many couples are afraid of letting go out of fear of loneliness, but on the other hand they are unwilling to put in the necessary work to make crucial changes. They can be stuck in a pattern that has no end. It takes serious soul-searching to honestly explore whether your relationship is worth saving. This test asks the hard questions and will hopefully lead to other thoughtful ones. After tallying your score, sit with the analysis for a while. Go back over your answers to find the biggest problems. Then decide if you want to try to work it out. In some cases, it might mean fighting to save your relationship against all odds. If that's the case, ask yourself what you have to lose—and what can be gained.

1 Do you get along better when you're apart?

a. Yes

b. Sometimes

c. No

2 Your partner tells you he's working late. You:

a. Think he's lying.

b. Believe he might be lying

c. Trust him.

3 Would you say you still like your partner as a friend?

a. No

b. Sometimes

c. Yes

4 You're both at a restaurant with a group of friends. He says something insulting to you. Your reaction?

a. You yell at him in front of the others.

b. You say nothing until you get home and then let him have it!

c. You ask him in a calm voice in front of everyone to apologize because he hurt your feelings.

5 Is sex still good?

a. No

b. Sometimes

c. Yes

6 Have either of you ever been physically or emotionally abusive with each other?

a. Yes

b. Once

c. Never

7 If you open up and tell your partner about a problem you're having, he is likely to:

a. Continue whatever he's doing.

b. Give you his standard answer.

c. Listen and offer sage advice.

8 Have either of you ever cheated?

a. Yes—more than once

b. Once

c. Never

9 Your partner suggests a weekend getaway. You:

a. Are revolted by the suggestion.

b. Think it may help to work stuff out.

c. Get excited about the idea.

10 Do you share a history of little white lies?

a. Yes

b. Well, just a few

c. No

11 If your partner was flirting with a good friend, you would most likely:

a. Pretend to ignore it. Really . . . who cares?

b. Tell them to knock it off.

c. Ask your partner about it later and let him know how weird it made you feel.

12 Do you still find him attractive?

a. No

b. Sometimes

c. Yes!

13 Do you get along with each other's families?

a. No

b. Mostly

c. Yes

14 When you and your partner argue, you:

a. Both scream until your voices are hoarse.

b. Yell for a while but calm down. One of you apologizes eventually.

c. Take turns hearing the other one out.

15 Are you feeling bored with the relationship?

a. Yes

b. Sometimes

c. No

16 Do you fantasize about being with someone else?

a. Yes

b. Sometimes

c. No

17 Your partner has done something that deeply offends you.
How long is it likely you'll hold on to it—and throw it back in his face?

a. Forever!

b. Until the pain goes away.

c. About a week. I try to let it go.

18 Would you be willing to go to couples therapy to make changes in
the way you treat each other?

a. No

b. Maybe for a brief time

c. Yes—for as long as it takes

19 Do you think it's possible that your partner can really change?

a. No

b. Maybe

c. Yes

20 If your partner wasn't feeling well, you would:

a. Get annoyed.

b. Ask him once what you can get for him.

c. Give him unlimited TLC.

21 Do you think if you broke up, you would get back together again?

a. No

b. Maybe

c. Probably

22 Is it true that one of the biggest reasons you're still hanging on is because you're afraid to be alone?

a. Yes

b. Maybe

c. No

23 Do your friends or family advise you to leave him?

a. Yes

b. On occasion

c. No

24 Do either of you have a drug or alcohol problem?

a. Yes

b. Not really

c. Definitely not

25 Would you be willing to try anything to save this relationship?

a. No

b. It depends

c. Yes

Analysis

MOSTLY A'S
YOUR RELATIONSHIP NEEDS A LOT OF WORK.

Here's the bottom line: Does your relationship make you a better person? Or does it lead you to feel badly about yourself? Does it inspire you to make the most out of yourself? Or does it coerce you into doing things you would rather not do? In other words, is your relationship tapping into your higher self? Well, if you received this score, chances are the answer is no. And this is the essential point. A good relationship should compliment you—not suck the life out of you. It should offer you hope, and even more crucially, make you happy. If instead, your relationship is consistently making you miserable and yet there's still a voice inside of you screaming out "But I love him! I love him!" then you need to dig deeper.

ADVICE

· Make two lists. Write down everything right about the relationship. On the other one, write down everything wrong. Which list is longer? Are there crucial areas where either of you consistently fall short? Is there a pattern? Do you think you can change your behavior? Do you think he can change his?
· Be honest and explore why you're afraid to leave him. Ask yourself: "What's the worst thing that could happen if we split up?" Allow yourself to envision what life would be like if he was no longer a part of it. Is your life better, or is it unbearable?
· Write a letter to yourself. Be kind and gentle. Tell yourself how much you love yourself. Explore the reasons why you deserve happiness. Discover your strengths and forgive your weaknesses. Acknowledge your past mistakes with understanding. Be sure to write about the future you envision.

MOSTLY B'S
YOUR RELATIONSHIP CAN USE SOME TWEAKING.

Your relationship may be going through a rough patch, but the basic foundation is sound. You've had hard times lately, and you're feeling uneasy and maybe resentful. Still, by the looks of it, this relationship is worth saving. Just because you may hit a few bumps in the road and things might not always look so rosy doesn't automatically mean that you can't work it out. As long as you are realistic with yourself and your partner, you'll be able to repair the damage. But it's up to *you*. Begin by asking yourself whether you're willing to invest energy into making it a better relationship. If you still look forward to spending time together, the answer is probably yes. From here, you'll need to make a few adjustments.

ADVICE

- Schedule time to be a duo. Of course you're both very busy and that's part of the problem. It seems the only time you get together is for chores. Make sure you also have time to have fun and be carefree and romantic—at least once a week.
- Ask yourself: Is he my rock? Remind yourself that your partner has been with you through tough times, maybe the death of a loved one, a job loss, or your own illness. Can you still lean on him? If the answer is yes, consider him a keeper.
- Clear the air. Maybe your partner is harboring some ill will that hasn't been expressed, or you're resentful and it's coming out in odd places. Time for a talk. But before you begin, set ground rules: no yelling or blaming. Set aside enough time, in a place where you won't be disturbed, to really air grievances. Stay calm and listen to his side of the story. Ask for the same in return. When you've both shared your grievances, kiss and make up.

MOSTLY C'S
YOU'RE IN GREAT SHAPE.

Whether you've been together for years, or you're a fairly new match, your love is very much alive and thriving. Sure, you have some down days, or some really boring ones, but who doesn't? The point is, you can see yourself with this person for the rest of your life. You love the sound of his voice and the feel of his skin. You respect his point of view and know he feels the same way about you. Trust? You have it, but neither of you takes the other for granted. As partnerships go, yours is a darn good one. But there are a couple of things you can do to make it even better.

ADVICE

- Laugh together. Sharing a sense of humor makes the hard times more bearable.
- Share a hobby. It can be tennis, biking, dancing, hiking, camping—even antiques shopping for a stamp collection. The point is to spend relaxing time together. Studies show couples who share a hobby rank their relationship as happiest.
- Keep flirting. It's the absolute best way to maintain your high-octane mutual attraction.

Exercise

Keep eye contact. Softly gaze into each other's eyes. Without speaking, allow your thoughts to flow. Keep your feelings present and your body's sensations open. Encourage a feeling of oneness.

"True love begins when nothing
is looked for in return."

—ANTOINE DE SAINT-EXUPÉRY

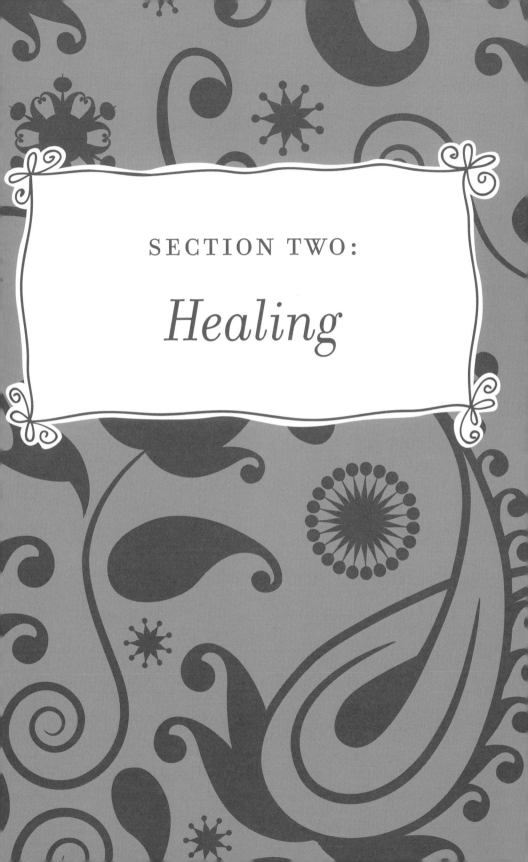

SECTION TWO:

Healing

Chapter Four:
Affirmations

Affirmations are a powerful tool to help couples change the way they perceive themselves separately and as members of their relationship. Affirmations work by using repetition to change the subconscious mind. Imagine this: Your mind is a control board of thoughts and feelings; the subconscious is the big switch in charge of it all. Turn it one way and you're on cloud nine, turn it another and you're down in the dumps. For example, if you say things like, "This will never work," "I'm so unlovable," "Our relationship is horrible," or "He's a jerk!" your thoughts, even the subconscious ones, turn into self-fulfilling prophecies. However, in the same vein, by using positive affirmations, you can instill constructive and loving thoughts in your mind. After all, energy follows thought. That's why affirmations like, "We can make this work," "We're on the right track," "He's really trying," and "I'm loveable" can turn your relationship from a dark, troubled, and hopeless place toward an arena of light, change, and hope.

Some people believe that it's necessary to repeat affirmations aloud hundreds of times a day. I'm not one of those people. If you are expounding aloud on positive aspects of your relationship, but inwardly hearing yourself tear down your partner, relationship, or self, your internal voice will win out. That's why I strongly believe that the most effective affirmations are those repeated internally when you are in a peaceful or quiet state while meditating, walking, watching the clouds, or simply lying on the bed or couch. The trick is to say affirmations while your mind is in a relaxed and receptive state, what scientists refer to as traveling on "alpha brain waves."

It's best to keep your affirmations in the present with statements such as "I am happy," rather than "I am going to be happy." It's also a good idea to avoid any negative words; frame your affirmations to reflect what you want rather than what you fear or dread or dislike. For example, instead of the affirmation "I wish I were less self-conscious," opt for "I am confident." Also, avoid putting your affirmations on a deadline. "Our relationship will be healed in month," means you're leaving yourself open for failure. Simply say, "Our relationship is healing."

Personally created affirmations are optimal, but the ones listed below are also strong and effective. In any case, make sure to pick affirmations that resonate like a vibrating bell within your being—not just from your logical mind. To help affirmations reach their most powerful potential, you can try visualizations to accompany them. For example, you might imagine your lover in your arms, walking side by side with him and smiling, staring into each other's eyes, or both reaching for a shiny key or brilliant flickering star. The picture is ultimately your creation, so be the Rembrandt of romance.

Relationship Affirmations

- Our relationship is strong and committed.
- We are in a fulfilling and nurturing relationship.
- Our relationship is honest, loyal, and trusting.
- We are in a loving relationship.
- We are compatible spiritually, physically, emotionally, and intellectually.
- My partner is the love of my life.
- We draw love and romance into our beings.
- All difficulties between my partner and myself are healing now.
- All of the changes in our relationship are for the best.
- We express pure, unconditional love toward each other.
- My partner finds me irresistible, and I find my partner irresistible.
- We choose to see each other's unconditional love and compassion.
- We forgive each other.

- We are in a joyous relationship.
- We are grateful for our love.
- We laugh together.
- All is well in our relationship.
- There is no problem we can't solve together.
- Our hearts are open to each other.
- Our relationship is working.
- We have a beautiful future together.
- We feel safe and protected by our love.
- We are attracted to each other.
- Our vision of the future is with each other.
- We are continually opening up to love and passion.
- We are good friends.
- We are receptive to our passions and sexual desires for each other.
- We support each other.
- We respect and accept our differences.
- We want to know how we can love each other more.
- We know true love opens new possibilities.
- When we look in each other's eyes we see love looking back.
- There is no end to our love.
- We rejoice in our relationship.
- We respect each other.
- We are focusing on the big picture.

Personal Affirmations

- Love is all around me. I feel it everywhere.
- I deserve love.
- I am strong, yet vulnerable and loving.
- I feel sexual pleasure.
- I embrace happiness.
- I attract loving relationships.
- I am now in the kind of relationship I want.
- The more I love myself, the more I love my partner.
- I am open to receiving love.
- Giving my partner unconditional love makes me happy.
- I love to see my partner happy.
- I possess inner strength.
- I am receptive to all the love my partner offers me.
- I release the illusion of control.
- I am receptive to my partner's romantic advances.
- I release drama from my life.
- I am living an authentic life.
- I choose people in my life who are kind, upbeat, and trustworthy.
- I am grateful for all the relationships in my life.
- I stay open to life's possibilities.
- I let go of preconceptions.
- I attract inspiration in my life.

After Affirmations

Allow fifteen minutes to remember as many happy memories of time spent together that you can conjure up (maybe write your recollections in your journal). Don't limit yourself. Go all the way back to the beginning of the relationship, when your eyes first locked or you shared your first kiss or tender embrace. Allow yourself to recall all the significant and not-so-significant moments when you felt passionate, put down your defenses and let yourself go completely, laughed together, cried in each other's arms, talked and listened intently throughout the night, traveled to an exotic place together, or rolled down a hill and got up giddy and feeling free. Remember when you sang together, celebrated a happy event, or enjoyed an exquisite meal. In other words, don't censor your happy memories; call them forth. Get all your senses involved. Try to remember how he smelled, what he was wearing, how he felt, the sound of his voice, the music playing in the background, the touch of the breeze on your skin, the flavor of his kiss, the tickle in your ear when he whispered your name—remember how he touched you so deeply. Immerse yourself in the picture of your passion.

Chapter Five: Wish Lists

What Is a Wish List?

When we write our thoughts down we make them clearer and firmer. This is especially true when it comes to our intentions and goals. That's why it's common for relationship experts to ask couples to create a "Wish List." It's a way of creating a mental blueprint of your ideal relationship. This can include traits, dynamics, hopes and aspirations, things you want to change, and stuff you wish you could set free. Anything that you believe will make your relationship stronger, more enjoyable, open, and enduring. Keep this list handy; whenever you get the inspiration, you can add to it.

Remember, you can make any wish you want. But don't forget—wishes really do come true, so be sure to ask for things you truly want. And then, believe with all your heart that you'll get it. One caveat: Don't bother wishing for something in the past to change. For example, "I wish we didn't fight about last night's dinner." Forget it. What's done is done. Instead, focus on a new, healing future together, and begin again.

A Head Start

Here are some wishes to help you get the hang of it. But, of course, it's best to create your own wish list, one that comes straight from *your* heart.

- I wish we could go on a romantic retreat.
- I wish for more financial security.
- I wish we enjoyed a hobby together.
- I wish we spent more time together.
- I wish we were more considerate of each other.
- I wish we would argue less.
- I wish we could work better as a team to get things done—like cleaning the house.
- I wish we were less critical of each other.
- I wish we had a stress-free life.
- I wish we had more time to relax.
- I wish we laughed more.
- I wish we could be totally honest with each other.
- I wish we could spend the day in bed making love.

Your Wish List

Reflections

WHICH OF YOUR WISHES HAVE ALREADY COME TRUE?

Relationship experts remind us that often we wish for what we already have. Sit quietly for a few minutes and then think about what you think you want, and if you may already have it. Allow gratitude to take the place of your yearning.

_____

_____

_____

_____

_____

_____

_____

_____

_____

_____

_____

_____

_____

_____

_____

_____

_____

_____

_____

_____

_____

_____

_____

_____

_____

WHAT ARE YOU WISHING FOR
THAT YOU MIGHT NOT REALLY WANT?

Remember the wise adage: "Be careful what you wish for because it may come true." Allow yourself to imagine what life would be like if your wishes really did come true. You might want to revise your list. This exercise helps to clarify what you really want in your relationship and what you need to focus on in your life.

_____

_____

_____

_____

_____

_____

_____

_____

_____

_____

_____

_____

_____

_____

_____

_____

_____

_____

_____

Chapter Six:
The Power Of Tens

Ten Ways to Tell How Much He Cares

1. He wants to spend time around you. Lots of time.

2. He teases you.

3. He contacts you at least once during the day.

4. He asks your opinion.

5. He gives you plenty of compliments.

6. He buys you gifts you really want.

7. He gives you plenty of physical affection.

8. He doesn't get defensive if you disagree with him.

9. He introduces you to everyone in his world, from family to friends.

10. He takes you to places that mean something special to him.

Ten Ways to Show You Really Care

1. _____

_____

2. _____

_____

3. _____

_____

4. _____

_____

5. _____

_____

6. _____

_____

7. _____

_____

8. _____

_____

9. _____

_____

10. _____

_____

Ten Ways to Ruin a Relationship

How many can you claim? How many can your partner claim? By naming and acknowledging your actions—you can change them.

1. Do you neglect your partner?
2. Do you withhold sex or other physical expressions of love?
3. Do you cheat on your lover—or are you deceitful in other ways?
4. Do you attack your partner by being emotionally, or even physically, abusive?
5. Do you use your partner as a scapegoat or to take out your frustrations? Do you blame your lover for your faults or problems?
6. Do you nag or nitpick?
7. Do you try to control your lover with a "my way or the highway" attitude?
8. Do you inhabit negativity and cloud your partner's view?
9. Do you always put yourself first? Or . . .
10. Do you always put yourself last (which can lead to resentment, bitterness, or anger)?

Ten Ways to Be Romantic

1. Write a love poem.
2. Hold hands in public.
3. Dedicate a song on the radio.
4. Take a bubble bath together.
5. Offer a back massage.
6. Write "I love you" on the bathroom mirror with lipstick or through steam.
7. Leave a love note in the car.
8. Give a blank check for kisses.
9. Toss rose petals on the bed.
10. Make a CD of love songs.

Ten Ways to Be Happy

1. Let go of perfection. Nobody is perfect and nothing in life is either.

2. Release comparisons. Don't measure your life or your relationship with those of others. Be content with your own life.

3. Take time out for yourself, whether it's walking in the park, working on a hobby, meditating, yoga, or pampering yourself with a bath.

4. Give yourself a music break. Stop what you're doing and tune in.

5. Nurture friendships outside your relationship.

6. Dance.

7. Be grateful for your life.

8. Volunteer. Helping others gives immense satisfaction and happiness. Make someone's life more beautiful by contributing in your own small way.

9. Try to stay in the present—without worrying about the future or regretting your past.

10. Find something funny. Deep belly laughs release feel-good endorphins and even boost the immune system.

Chapter Seven: Illuminations

Although there are exercises following each quiz, the techniques described in this chapter explore different avenues to understanding yourself, your partner, and your relationship through the use of ancient wisdom. The techniques have been simplified and updated to make them more accessible. But don't be fooled by their simplicity—the lessons learned can be transformative.

Facial Reading

Some features are classically handsome or beautiful, others more exotically lovely—still others are less appealing. But every face is a map revealing what lies beneath. It's not just the eyes that are windows to the soul. The way your eyes are spaced, your mouth is sized, and how your hair is shaped all reveal deep insights into your own and your partner's true nature.

Get a photograph of yourself and of your partner. Study the photographs, then read the analysis below and take notes. After careful consideration, you'll know a lot about who you really are and who your partner truly is.

PLACE A PHOTOGRAPH OF YOURSELF IN THE BOX.

You

PLACE A PHOTOGRAPH OF YOUR PARTNER IN THE BOX.

Your Partner

HAIR

Hair is more than a woman's crowing glory; it's a measure of strength and endurance. If your partner's hair is fine and silky it means he's sensitive and perhaps, emotionally fragile. If it's thick and bristly it reflects physical strength and his ability to rebound from life's inevitable pressures.

FOREHEAD

When the forehead is large it reflects idealism, while if it's low it can mean a lack of confidence. Often those with an overdeveloped crown are more authoritarian, while a narrow one can indicate passivity. A short head may indicate a more spontaneous nature, while a longer or wider one means thoughtfulness and a measured response to conflict.

THE EYES

Eyes that aren't set evenly may mean your lover has the ability to see things from different perspectives and has the ability to solve problems by thinking things through and coming up with original solutions.

If the eyes slant upward (cat eyes), this person knows how to grab hold of opportunities and get exactly what he or she wants. Some may interpret this as having a devious nature—but that's not necessarily so. Use your experience to interpret this physical characteristic.

But be cautious if your lover's eyes slant downward. This often means the person has a hard time saying no and can find themselves in compromising positions, like being unable to deflect a flirt.

How far or wide apart are the eyes? If there's at least one eye width between the eyes, then your partner usually has good judgment and a clear view. The closer the eyes are set together, the narrower their opinions or views of the world. It's a strong indication there's a lack of sophistication and independence.

MOUTH

A large mouth with full lips means the individual is independent and able to speak their mind.

A person with a smaller than usual mouth is often more humble and needs support. They also shy away from the limelight.

If the ends of the mouth curve upward—as if in a smile—this individual attracts others and usually has a large circle of friends.

In contrast, the down-turned mouth can mean a difficult childhood and someone who tends to exaggerate or lie.

If a person has big Angelina Jolie lips it means freedom is cherished and nothing is held back. Although this individual is a powerful speaker who sounds convincing, in reality, when it comes to acting on their words: not so good.

Notes

ID the Shape of a Face

Reading the shape of faces to understand personality is an ancient Chinese practice and takes years of serious study to master. But you can still get invaluable insights just by studying the following basics:

ROUND

If the face is round or fleshy and has relaxed features, it indicates a person who is easygoing and usually accepts life as it comes. These are homebodies who enjoy good food, entertaining with flair, and welcoming family and friends to stay for weeks at a time. They are optimistic, generous souls who love a good time. What's the downside? Your partner is likely to extend invitations without consulting you. Plus, round face types have a tendency to procrastinate.

SQUARE

A square face with large, sharp, or strong features usually belongs to a person who loves freedom, enjoys travel, and is a real go-getter. This person has lots of ambition with energy to back it up. Square-faced individuals, in general, are the movers and shakers of the world, but they also possess a solid maternal or paternal streak. What's the downside? Square face types are big talkers. Sometimes you can't get a word in edgewise. Plus, they can be stubborn.

LONG

Usually long-faced individuals have delicate and graceful features as well as long and lean bodies. They have a tendency to need lots of recognition and go after it by accumulating money, power, or public recognition. Successful and competitive, they revel in the limelight. What's the downside? They hate to lose and can be ruthless. Plus, they often require a lot of attention and reassurance.

TRIANGULAR

With a wide forehead and pointed chin, triangular-faced people usually have thin bodies with willowy features. Reserved and quiet by nature, these folks are often deep thinkers who are honest perfectionists. They have a lot of integrity and will always seek the high road. Spiritual insight is often an ideal that is pursued with fervor. What's the downside? Triangular face types may be pensive and a little too quiet. Plus, their modesty means ambition is secondary. They often keep their accomplishments a secret.

BLUNTED TRIANGLE

The basic motivation of people with this shaped face is adventure. They represent the Chinese sign for fire. With a narrow forehead coming to a peak and a wide jaw and chin, the face and body are often skinny, pointed, wiry, and have quick features. What's the downside? These people, although talented and outgoing with a ton of vitality, can often be demanding and picky. Plus, they can be perfectionists.

Read What's Written on Your Partner's Palm

Every hand is unique. Perhaps that's why reading palms is an ancient tool used not only to understand the past and predict the future, but to comprehend a person's true nature. Of course, true palm reading takes a lifetime of study. However, this snapshot view will definitely give you insights into your lover's life.

HERE'S HOW TO DO IT—AND WHAT TO LOOK FOR:

Read both hands. One hand is known as the "active" hand and the other as the "passive." A right-handed person's active hand will be their right hand; the opposite is true for a left-handed individual.

In the passive hand you'll be able to find inherited traits and potential.

The active hand reveals changes to inherited traits.

Consider the size of the hand in relationship to the rest of the body. A large hand means the person spends more time thinking than doing—and a small hand in relationship to the body more often than not means the person spends more time doing rather than thinking about taking action.

Next consider the shape of the hand. There are four general shapes representing the four elements: air, earth, fire, and water.

Air hands have a square palm, long fingers, and thin, clear lines on the palm. A person with this hand is often restless, needs change, is social, and loves to be challenged mentally. Although likely to be true-blue, they tend to be flirts.

Earth hands are square with shorter fingers, thick skin, and deep, clear, straight lines on the palms. This person is down-to-earth, practical, reliable, and trustworthy. If your lover has this shape palm, there's a good chance they won't cheat. (They may not be that exciting, either.)

Fire hands have long palms, short fingers, and lots of lines. The palms usually feel firm and are warm more often than not. Although people with these kinds of hands love a risk, they're also positive and confident—and don't need to have fling to feel good about themselves.

Water hands are all about length: long fingers and palms and plenty of fine lines. The skin is soft and often damp. These are the hands of a person who is creative, emotional, and needy. Vulnerable and sensitive, an individual with water hands often needs a lot of TLC.

The Palm Lines

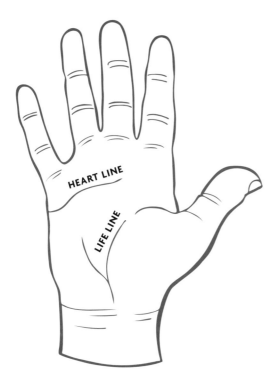

HEART LINE

LIFE LINE

Note: The palm is made up of major, secondary, and minor lines. A palm with lots of fine lines and major lines is a sensitive and complicated individual prone to worry and stress. In fact, the fewer the lines, the more straightforward—and easy to read—the individual is.

THE HEART LINE

The highest major line in the palm is the heart line. If the line is high, chances are the person is not only passionate but also high-strung and jealous. A Heart Line that stretches completely across the hand indicates an individual who is in-check emotionally. They hold back rather than give. A heart line that curves up toward the index finger belongs to a person who is tender, warmhearted, and affectionate. Any crosses or breaks in the Heart Line indicate times of sadness or complication in relationships.

THE LIFE LINE

The curved line that swings from near the base of the palm (by the wrist) to between the thumb and first finger is the life line. When it comes to matters of the heart, a wide life line usually means the person is generous, compassionate, and easily able to love. However, a life line that is close to the thumb shows a person who may find it difficult to give of their time and their feelings as well.

THE MARRIAGE LINE

These lines reside right above the heart line. Light, fine horizontal lines show that the relationship my not be worthy of commitment. One obvious and long line suggests a relationship that is long-term, happy, and committed. When there is more than one long, deep line, the lower one is thought to describe the earlier relationship in the person's life.

Notes

The Body Language Checklist

No matter how long you've been a couple, there are certain physical signals that suggest whether your relationship is still vibrant. Next time you're out and about with your partner at a restaurant, party, or bar, use this checklist to see if he's still attracted to you. He:

· Holds your glance a little longer.
· Makes eye contact, looks away, and then glances again your direction.
· Touches you while he speaks.
· Leans in toward you.
· Swaggers or flexes his muscles. It seems corny, but this is an age-old display of masculinity—like a peacock strutting its feathers.
· Smoothes his clothing or runs his hand through his hair.
· Speaks low so only you can hear, thus creating a bubble and making space for just the two of you.

Notes

Reading Feet

Even though palmistry is the more conventional way to get insights into your lover's nature, feet as well as the hands offer revealing clues:

- If there are darkened areas of skin on the toe pads, it means they've been walking on the front of their feet, which is often a sign of a low mood.
- A callus on the ball of the foot, just under the little toe, indicates that the person is shouldering too much responsibility.
- When an individual is embarrassed, the back of the big toe blushes red.
- The second toe on the right foot is like the palm—it reveals what someone wants in life. If it's being achieved, the toe will touch the floor.
- If there's a gap between the second and third toe, it indicates the person isn't connecting to their emotions.
- The fourth toe is directly connected to relationships. If there's involuntary twitching when you're talking about your relationship, it reveals discomfort.
- When a person's second toe is the longest, it indicates they need to feel in charge because they have naturally strong leadership qualities. Rulers from ancient Egypt and Hawaiian royalty reportedly all had long second toes.
- If the last joint of the third toe is at an angle, your partner has the ability to be duplicitous—and is often equally misunderstood. Remarkably, spies often have this trait.
- When the second toe on the left foot leans toward the big toe, it's a sign of someone who is sentimental. Guess which celebrity has this slanted toe: Reese Witherspoon.
- If your partner has an especially small little toe then there's a real sense of playfulness and fun.
- Little toe pointed at an angle? It's a sign of an unconventional nature. If it can be wiggled then the individual has a restless nature—and is prone to seek change.

SECTION THREE:

Journal

Chapter Eight:
Why Keep a Journal?

Here are just a few of the countless reasons that keeping a journal will improve not only your relationship, but your inner life.

- Journal writing helps us understand events that happen in our lives.
- Journal writing gives us the opportunity to be quiet, tune in to our thoughts, be open with our emotions, and release honest expression.
- Journal writing requires nothing elaborate. All you need is a notepad and a pen or pencil. You needn't be an accomplished writer or have any special abilities.
- Journal writing can help record events that take place before memory corrodes or embellishes them.
- Journal writing gives us the opportunity to work through feelings without harming anyone else—including oneself. It's best to set aside a specific time each day to write in a journal. Be consistent.
- Journal writing helps us pay attention to details. We often overlook the little events, but as the saying goes, "life is in the details." The more you use your mind and the more you pay attention to the events that occur, the easier it is to see them clearly.
- Journal writing allows us to view the issues in our life with a more keenly observant and less frantic perception.
- Journal writing allows us to let go of the issues that occur in our lives and instead place them in the notebook, ready to be dealt with when we are more capable or understanding.
- Journal writing allows us to honor all the events of the day—from the special to the mundane.

- Journal writing encourages us to feel gratitude and allows us to be free to express regret.
- Journal writing is personal. Don't worry about spelling, grammar, your handwriting, or whether you're Hemingway. Write from your heart.

Journal Pages

BIBLIOGRAPHY

Godek, Greg. *1001 Ways to Be Romantic: Now Completely Revised and More Romantic Than Ever*. Naperville: Sourcebooks, Inc., 2000.

Graman, Marilyn, and Walsh, Maureen. *There is No Prince and Other Truths Your Mother Never Told You: A Guide to Having the Relationship You Want*. New York: Life Works Books, 2003.

Koopersmith, Linda. *The Beverly Hills Organizer's Home Organizing Bible: A Pro's Answers to Your Organizing Prayers*. Gloucester: Fair Winds Press, 2005.

Bradberry, PhD, Travis, and Greaves, PhD, Jean. *The Emotional Intelligence Quick Book*. New York: Fireside, 2005.

Spiegel, Jill. *The Pocket Pep Talk*. Goal Getters, 1997.

Kirschner, PhD, Diana. *Opening Love's Door: The Seven Lessons*. Lincoln: iUniverse, Inc., 2004.

Butler, Gillian, and Hope, Tony. *Managing Your Mind: The Mental Fitness Guide*. New York: Oxford University Press, 2007.

Wood, Eve. *10 Steps to Take Charge of Your Emotional Life: Overcoming Anxiety, Distress, and Depression Through Whole-Person Healing*. New York: Hay House, 2007.

Straus, PhD, Martha. *Adolescent Girls in Crisis: Intervention and Hope*. New York: W. W. Norton & Company, Inc., 2007.